How to Turn $1 into $1 Million in Seven Years or Less

by

Roy McDonald

Copyright ©2006 Roy McDonald,

Copyright in individual quotes contained in this book remains with the copyright holder as attributed and where still current. All rights for the body of the text of this work reserved. Without limiting the rights under copyright reserved above, and apart from any fair dealing for the purposes of private study, research, criticism or review, no part of this publication may be reproduced, stored in or introduced into a retrieval system, or transmitted, in any form or by any means (electronic, mechanical, photocopying, or otherwise), without the prior written permission of the copyright holder, Roy McDonald, OneLife International Pty Limited.

ISBN 0-9751081-0-7

Disclaimer: OneLife International Pty Limited ACN 106 861 723 ("OL") is a corporate authorised representative of Financial Planning Works Pty Limited ACN 003 780 407 ("FPW") Australian Financial Services Licensee number 247180

OL and FPW, or any associates, speakers, facilitators or employees thereof present this publication as a general nature only. Professional advice relevant to your particular circumstances should always be sought by recipients before acting on the information contained in this publication and presentation.

While OL and FPW, or any associates, speakers, facilitators or employees thereof take all reasonable care in the production of this publication, OL and FPW, or any associates, speakers, facilitators or employees thereof accept no responsibility for any loss or damage of any kind suffered by a recipient relying on the content of this publication.

The information published and presented to you by OL and FPW, or any associates, speakers, facilitators or employees thereof is published in accordance with the conditions of the Licence. Investment in securities and derivatives involve risk. OL and FPW, or any associates, speakers, facilitators or employees thereof provide educational programs in a wide range of areas including the stock market, but do not provide through this publication, or otherwise, any investment, financial produce, legal or taxation advice as to the suitability of any products or services referred to in this publication for your particular objectives, financial situation or needs. Financial product and investment advice and examples given or described in this publication including forecasts and opinions are for general educational purposes only. Any testimonials or discussions are provided voluntarily, without payment, inducement or other benefit and are from genuine clients or students of OL and FPW, or any associates, speakers, facilitators or employees thereof. The examples, guidance and advice published in this publication have been prepared without taking into account your particular objectives, financial situation and needs, or of any other person. You should not make any investment in any financial product or service unless you have assessed the financial product or service yourself, or with the help of an Australian Financial Services Licensee or authorised representative of an Australian Financial Services Licensee. OL and FPW, or any associates, speakers, facilitators or employees thereof do not intend any information published to constitute advice and you should not rely upon, or assume, that any statement published constitutes any type of advice.

The information contained and presented in this book is for educational purposes only. OL and FPW, or any associates, speakers, facilitators or employees thereof are not stockbrokers, brokering agents, or registered investment advisors.

The purpose of this book is to furnish you with basic knowledge that you will be able to apply to various situations and transactions. OL and FPW, or any associates, speakers, facilitators or employees thereof do not guarantee any results or returns on business investments as the result of any actions taken, based on this information. It is recommended by OL and FPW, or any associates, speakers, facilitators or employees thereof to all clients that all forms of investment (without exception) carry some degree of risk (varying from minimal to high), and potential for loss of capital and independent advice should be obtained.

Certain stocks, options, managed investment funds, properties, etc will be mentioned during the program and in this manual, and this should be taken as purely for educational purposes, and (where appropriate) to illustrate certain financial principles or techniques. OL and FPW, or any associates, speakers, facilitators or employees thereof suggests that you obtain your own independent advice for your current needs and objectives.

OL and FPW, or any associates, speakers, facilitators or employees thereof recommend that you seek professional advice on any and all of your investment plans. However, OL and FPW, or any associates, speakers, facilitators or employees thereof do not recommend the retention of any specific financial professionals (brokers, etc) or any particular product. The mention of any such professional person, organisation or product during this program does not imply any endorsement or recommendation of that specific person, organisation or product by OL and FPW, or any associates, speakers, facilitators or employees thereof.

The content of this publication is copyright. Apart from any use permitted under the Copyright Act, no part may be reproduced by any process, or any other exclusive right exercised without the permission of OL and FPW, or any associates, speakers, facilitators or employees thereof.

Cover design / typesetting and layout by Musarra Media,
Surry Hills, Sydney Australia +612 9281 3644

First edition printed 2003
Second edition printed 2006
Third edition printed 2008

Contents

1. Introduction — 1
2. Five Forms of Income — 4
3. Strategic Spending — 12
4. The Wealth Account — 17
5. Taxation — 23
6. Provisional Tax — 28
7. Leverage — 35
8. Yield — 43
9. Strategic Plan — 46
10. Momentum Trading for Success — 50
11. Live Trading for Success — 60
12. The Six Masteries — 62
13. The Million Dollar Session — 67
14. Twelve Secrets of Wealth — 69
15. What Does Being Wealthy Mean to You? — 77
16. The First Wealth Strategy: Value Each Dollar — 79
17. The Magic Game of Golf — 81
18. The Second Wealth Strategy: Actively Manage Each Dollar — 87
19. Other Wealth Strategies — 90
20. Twelve False Wealth Assumptions — 95

21.	The Billion Dollar Success Plan	104
22.	Debt Free in Five Years—Financially Independent in a Further Seven Years	109
23.	Ten Commandments for Creating a Financial Fortress	113
24.	Preservation and Protection of Your Wealth	114
25.	Eight Principles of Wealth	116
26.	Five Secrets of Running your Own Business	122
27.	Own Your Business	125
28.	Five Magic Steps to Achieving Your Goals	130
29.	The Seven Year Plan	135
30.	Buying Real Estate	145
31.	Attitude	153
32.	Habits	156
33.	Self-Image	158
34.	Desire	159
35.	Change	163
36.	Creativity	166
37.	Confidence	171
38.	Seventeen Success Principles	177
39.	The Step-by-Step Approach to Turning $1 into $1Million in Seven Years or Less, $1 at a Time	178
40.	Summary	185
41.	Recommended Reading	188
42.	Programs Available	189
43.	Glossary	190
44.	Testimonials	192

Dedication

*This book is dedicated to my two special teachers
in the form of my two beautiful children,*

Harrison and Jessica.

                                    Roy McDonald,
                                    their grateful father.

Acknowledgments

I started business in 1968 and, in over 40 years of activity, I have learned a lot on the journey.

I am grateful for all the teachers who have passed my way. These have been in the guise of clients to team members, associates, employees past and present, lawyers, advisors and partners. They have come in all shapes and sizes, with many lessons for me to learn and I would like to thank them all.

At OneLife we have many people who have dedicated their lives to see to it that our business works and for this I will be forever grateful.

In the past 30-odd years, I have been in touch with over one million people through our programs and one- to-one meetings.

These people have all gone through their journey, supported not only by me, directly, but also our associates at Financial Management Works- Nick Stanton, Vigen Evanian, Peter Horsfield, Mark Sablatnig and their team.

It helps me go the extra mile for our clients when all these people work together as one, which they consistently do.

Overall, the most important direct contact with our

clients is through our OneLife team who, in their own journey, have grown and contributed so much.

To Claus Gerling, for his unique trading presentations and sense of humour; to Harry and Helen Charalmabous for sharing their experiences in property development, and for their support and friendship.

To Malcolm Green, property project manager and good friend, and his skilled team, who have completed many development and building projects to a high standard.

To my sister, Sally, and my big brothers Bruce and Ken who I love and know they love me. They have always been examples for me.

To my Mum and Dad who have now passed away, knowing they always did the best that they possibly could for all of us, and were great teachers.

Bill Wright - my partner for 30 years in the travel industry - and the associate directors connected with the business. Bill, particularly, taught me fairness, respect and integrity.

All the people I have learned from since the early days of Earl Nightingale - the first piece of magic information I think I ever received I learned from him - Dale Carnegie, Dr Wayne W Dyer, Deepak Chopra, Marianne Williams, Anthony Robbins, Robert Kiyosaki, Brad Sugars, Roger Hamilton, Echardt Tolle and to Brandon Bays and The Journey.

There are many more who have made a great contribution to me and for this I am truly grateful for all their teachings.

And lastly to my greatest teacher and love, Katrina McGilchrist who has been a shining light and a laser beam of truth and integrity to me. Her commitment to growth, compassion and contribution has been an inspiration to me and anyone who knows her.

Without her, this book could never have been written.

Where Are You Financially?

∼

'If you are not making the progress you would like and are capable of making, it is simply because your goals are not clearly defined.'

Paul J Meyer

1 Introduction

Congratulations on your decision to make a real difference in your life, financially.

If you follow the recipe I give you in this book, step by step, and undertake all the applications, the steps are simple. Your life will not only change financially, it will change your relationships, your health, and you will make a completely different contribution on this planet.

You have just begun a journey of momentous proportions. In this book I will take you on a step by step process of turning $1 into $1 million in seven years or less.

Many of our clients have achieved this feat. Although it is simple, it is not easy.

I am so excited about sharing this material with you, and I know one thing absolutely for certain—this book can change your life forever.

I know that is a very simple thing to say; and, it is true. If you follow the recipe I am going to give you in this book, step by step, and undertake all the applications (which, as I said earlier, are simple), your life will not only change financially, it will change your relationships, your health, and you will make a completely different contribution on this planet.

This book contains seven magic keys that will open seven magic locks, that will open seven magic doors, that will move your life to a completely new level. You will experience abundance at a level only dreamed of by most people.

> **'It is not enough to take steps which may some day lead to a goal; each step must be itself a goal and a step likewise.'**
> **Goethe**

We need all the doors open so the light can come through. Some of you have already opened some of these doors. Some of you have tried the locks and cannot get them to work. Some cannot get the keys to fit. Some people have no idea what I am talking about.

I believe there are no accidents in life, and choosing this book is part of your destiny in moving you forward.

Through the various chapters, you will sometimes be tempted to rush ahead to briefly read the content and not really study the material, or do the exercises that are intended.

I want to particularly ask that you work this book like you would a recipe and take each step one by one.

It's like baseball—you cannot get to second base if you haven't been to first. You cannot get to third unless you've been to first and second, and you can't get home unless you go first, second, third, home.

If you want to cut the corner, just jump up and down and you will find you are already at home base, without going anywhere. It's just that you will never achieve anything.

There are five important ingredients to this book that need to be digested, among other things, to have you become financially independent.

The first of these is to create five forms of income.

The second ingredient is to create a system so that you can be strategic with your spending.

The third is to deal with the issues of taxation, so that you minimise your taxation contribution, and thus enhance the available cash you have to invest and spend.

The fourth ingredient is to create leverage. This to enable you to create loan facilities or gearing[1] to enhance the yield on your investments

The fifth is to create a higher return on the investments that you make, by being smarter with those investments.

I will cover these matters in detail in individual chapters, so that you will fully understand their implication. Once brought together and actioned they make a formidable success story.

Remember, in your decisions is your destiny; this decision to proceed on this journey is the journey less travelled. Fewer than five per cent of the population would even want to buy this book or utilise its contents.

So, let's agree, you are a success already by the very investment in this process.

Once again, congratulations!

So, let's begin the journey.

2   Five Forms of Income

Ninety five per cent of our population at age 65 are dead, dead broke, or on the pension.

That is an extraordinary number, given we spend billions of dollars educating people from school days to retirement so that, at the end of the day, they can barely feed themselves on about $300 per week. This is assuming that they get a pension from either the government or a superannuation fund.

The pension has been transferred from the government's responsibility, in a lot of cases, to private enterprise, which is being made to put money away on behalf of its employees so that there is a fund available to deliver the pension. If you follow all the rules, this will be equivalent to approximately $300 per week.

If you receive more than this, generally your fund will be penalised by some tax treatment, such that you will pay extra tax for receiving this benefit.

The question stands to be answered, 'Why are ninety five percent of our population at age 65 dead, dead broke, or on the pension?'

In my seminars, I constantly get people saying things like, 'Well, it's the government's fault.'

A young man will raise his hand and say, 'I was brought up to believe that I was going to become a pensioner.'

A lady raises her hand and says, 'I was too frightened to invest.'

An older man yells out from the back, 'They fail to plan.'

The audience nods.

A young married couple says, 'It's very hard to save and build a financial future with children and expenses. By the time you educate your children and try to pay the mortgage off, there is not much left to invest.'

> 'The only people who think more about money than the rich are the poor.'
> Oscar Wilde

From the middle of the audience, a young man raises his hand and says, 'I am a student at university and in all the years from primary school to university I have been taught to get a job and to swap my life for money—no one has taught me how to be financially intelligent.'

A silence falls over the room.

I focus my attention on the young man and say to him, 'Have you read the book Rich Dad Poor Dad?' He nods.

I ask the audience, 'Who else has read that book?', and invariably twenty - thirty per cent of the participants will raise their hands.

I then go on to say, 'That book is an extraordinary book and a No. 1 best seller around the world, written by Robert Kiyosaki.'

To paraphrase the content of the book (by the way, I recommend you buy that book and read it), Robert had a rich dad and a poor dad.

His real dad was his poor dad who was a school teacher.

> **Your life is a perfect reflection of your beliefs. When you change your deepest beliefs about the world, your life changes accordingly.**

His poor dad told him to go to school, get good grades, work as hard as he could and - when he passed his exams - to write the best resume he could to get the best job he could; once achieved, work his way up the ladder, buy a house, pay it off and then he would be alright.

His father failed to add, 'and then you become a pensioner like I am going to become.' That is exactly what his father became.

Robert had a very good friend who had a rich dad.

He spent a lot of time with his friend. His friend's rich dad said to him, 'Yes, go to school and get good grades. Do not write a resume, write a business plan. There are a lot of 95-percenters out there who will want to work for you. These people are very frightened. On a Friday afternoon, a hand will come out and shake, looking for wages to fill it. Like heroin addicts, they are addicted to wages and they know no other way of creating income. These lovely people are three pays away from bankruptcy and they are caught up in the trap, swapping their lives for money.'

Quiet falls over the seminar room as these ideas settle in and I ask participants, 'Who is following what I am saying?' Most hands go up.

I then ask the student, 'So, why did you come tonight?'

He says, 'I know there is a better way. I love learning things but I don't want to repeat what my mother and father did, spending their entire lives working to save for a pension that can barely keep them alive. Every day I see fear in their faces and I don't want to have a family with my wife and children experiencing that kind of existence.'

I thank him and we acknowledge his contribution by giving him a round of applause as I believe the entire audience feels the same way.

We start with the first proposition.

As you will see in Figure 1, the P.A.Y.G., pay-as-you-go has a J.O.B., just-over-broke. Ninety-five per cent of our population operates, financially, in this area, either in this form or the form below it, called the sole trader.

The sole trader is a person who has a small business, consultancy, doctor, lawyer, candlestick maker.

It could be a mum and dad operation or a single operator, or a small activity where the proprietor or owner works in the business, and really what she, too, has is a J.O.B.

You will notice in Figure 1 there is a wall of F.E.A.R.

I call this wall of F.E.A.R the wall that must be crossed. F.E.A.R is *False Evidence Appearing Real*.

On the other side of this wall there is a business owner, and underneath that an investor.

A business owner is a person who has a business that works without him or her.

> **Doing what you love is not a recipe for an easier life, it is a recipe for an interesting life. Most likely you'll take on more responsibilities and more problems!**

Some people get confused and think they have a business when they are really a sole trader or a small business operator.

Michael Gerber from the *E-Myth* often uses an example to establish which one you operate; if you have a business, you should be able to pick up the phone and call your office or company and say, 'This is me, I won't be in for three months', and hang up. In three months' time, call into the office and if the business is still working, then you have a business.

If it's your wife on the phone saying, 'We need you', then what you really have is a job. You are working for the worst boss in the world; yourself.

If they don't know who is on the end of the line, you are in real trouble.

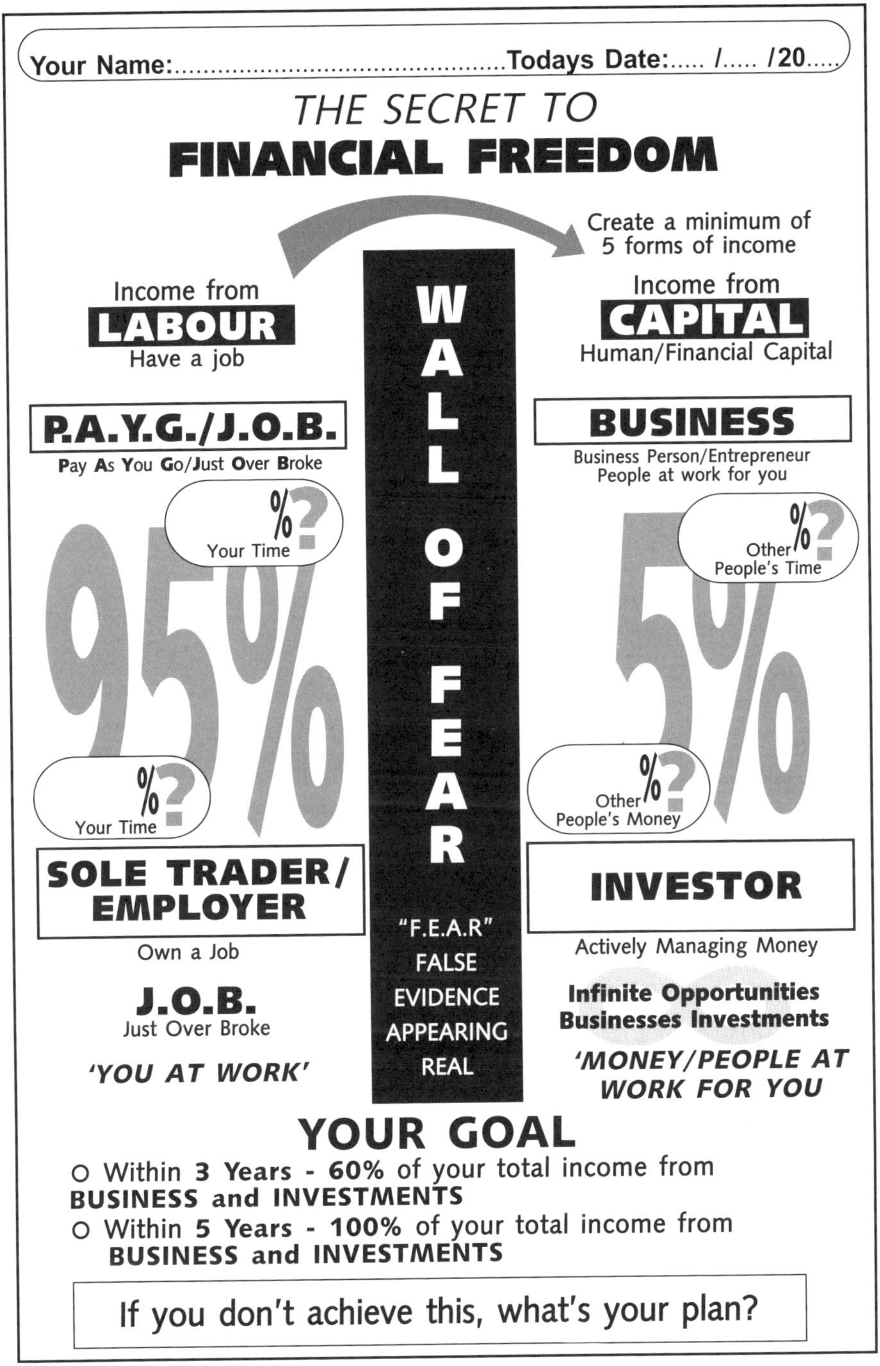

Your Name:... Todays Date:...../...../20.....

THE SECRET TO
FINANCIAL FREEDOM

Create a minimum of 5 forms of income

Income from LABOUR
Have a job

Income from CAPITAL
Human/Financial Capital

WALL OF FEAR

P.A.Y.G./J.O.B.
Pay As You Go/Just Over Broke

Your Time %?

95%

Your Time %?

SOLE TRADER/ EMPLOYER
Own a Job

J.O.B.
Just Over Broke

'YOU AT WORK'

BUSINESS
Business Person/Entrepreneur
People at work for you

Other People's Time %?

5%

Other People's Money %?

INVESTOR
Actively Managing Money

Infinite Opportunities Businesses Investments

'MONEY/PEOPLE AT WORK FOR YOU'

"F.E.A.R"
FALSE
EVIDENCE
APPEARING
REAL

YOUR GOAL

○ Within **3 Years** - **60%** of your total income from **BUSINESS and INVESTMENTS**
○ Within **5 Years** - **100%** of your total income from **BUSINESS and INVESTMENTS**

If you don't achieve this, what's your plan?

Figure 1

An investor is someone who has investments producing income and growth. These investments could be real estate, shares (equities), fixed term securities, debentures, collectibles, cfds, options, warrants—a whole host of various securities.

I ask the audience, 'How many jobs can you have at once?'

There is a thinking process going on and puzzled looks. I explain that at one time in my life I had four different jobs—one regular week day job, a weekend job and two separate night jobs.

I ask the audience, 'How many of you have had two or more jobs in your life at one time?' About 60 per cent of the audience raises their hands, which is typical of the commitment people make to try and get ahead.

I ask the question, 'How long can you sprint for?'

Laughter, 'Not long.'

'How many businesses can you have?'

A number of people respond, 'An infinite number.'

'How many investments can you have?'

'An infinite number.'

Those investments—in property, fixed securities, equities and endless combinations—can produce growth and passive forms of income so *you* don't work.

MONEY WORKS *FOR* YOU.

The goal is to have, within three years, 60 per cent of your income being generated from businesses or investments and, within five years, 100 per cent of your income passively being created from growth and income producing investments and businesses.

Over a five year period, the intention is to take an extra day off per week each year, reducing your time so that you are working only at the roles you are absolutely passionate about.

The five forms of income is not a 'get-rich-quick' scheme. It's a 'get-wealthy-slowly-and-keep-it' program—the first major step in producing income without swapping your life for money.

It's a program that needs to get started as soon as possible and can be achieved within five years, adding a new income stream each year.

> **Follow your heart. Your mission in life is not to be without problems—your mission is to get excited and embrace them as challenges.**

So, let's summarise what we have covered so far.

The important points to remember are:
- Five forms of income—a new income stream each year.
- Reduce your work by one day a week each year over five years.
- Work *on* your business, not *in* it.
- Adopt the habits of the rich and successful.

3 Strategic Spending

Being more efficient and effective with your money. Strategic Spending is the second magic formula for arranging your affairs.

You notice it's called *Strategic Spending*. It's not a budget. Budgets don't work. Neither do DIEts.

Strategic Spending is about creating a system to plan your expenses and take charge of your money, so that you will end up with ten per cent of your income, as a minimum, being saved in a Wealth Account to create wealth for your future.

> **In order to have something in your life, and keep it, you have to be comfortable with it. To make money—and keep it—you must be comfortable with money!**

Strategic Spending works because you are putting a strategy in for your future, and you are planning a year ahead for what you want to do. Ninety per cent of your bills are able to be planned, fairly accurately.

The reason why a lot of people fail to achieve their goals in life is that they have never really set them in the first place.

One of those important goals is to spend *less* than you earn. Ninety-five per cent of our population spends *all* they earn or *more* than they earn.

Less than five per cent of the population saves ten per cent or more of their income on a regular basis.

Most of us know how much we earn each year, but have little idea what we *spend* the money on. Like every successful business, we need to monitor income and expenditure while also ensuring that we are making a profit—in other words, saving some money.

The reason the strategic system was put in place was to get you ready for your business building plans.

If you can't be strategic about your spending and record it accordingly, there is no way in the long term that you can really build a business.

Unfortunately, most people take their poor habits of personal spending into their businesses and this is reflected in their failures.

Have the discipline to do little things you don't like, and you can spend your life doing the big things you do like.

Eighty percent of all small businesses go out of business within the first five years. Of the twenty per cent who make it through, eighty per cent of them go out of business in the next five years.

My experience tells me that the majority of the people who fail do so because there are certain areas that they are not good at, and one of them is often their inability to be strategic with their spending.

To access our Strategic Spending system, go to the OneLife website at *www.onelife.com.au/freedom* and download the sheets for the yearly planner and the monthly planner.

In the yearly planner, you will see that there are two basic pages starting with income for the spouse and the main provider, with a 12 month plan in advance.

It then moves on to saving a minimum of ten per cent of that income, and then down to paying for the basic essentials of food and out-of-pocket expenses. It then goes through to the third account—the operations account—all your costs of housing, transport, holidays, loans etc.

At the bottom of the second page you will find that the income and expenses are taken one from the other and added up monthly, showing either a positive or a negative balance and, ultimately, added up as a total for the year.

Next is the monthly section with 4 or 5 weeks in it. Fill it in exactly the same as you would the yearly one, starting with the current month.

Where should you begin? Right where you are—next month as you plan spending. Start right where you are.

At this point I usually get comments such as 'this is going to take a long time' and 'anyway it won't be very accurate as I have to guess'.

I agree this takes time and is only an estimation; and, if you are serious about your wealth you need to take charge of your spending.

It doesn't take that long. What you need to do is offset the time involved—an hour or two—for both you and your spouse, against what it will cost you later in life if you don't do it.

As far as the accuracy is concerned, it's better to be a little inaccurate than have nothing, because that would be total guess work.

What I am surprised to discover is that often the figures generated in this exercise are within ten per cent of the actual figures and, with the pluses and minuses involved, they often work out even more accurately.

The only thing you can guarantee about Strategic Spending is that it is wrong. However, it will give you the information and control that you will need to move yourself to the next stage.

It is very important to stop reading this book now and get onto the web and fill this in.

If you cannot do this right now and prefer to read on, make a definite time when you will sit down with your spouse - or if you are single, by yourself - and really complete this strategic spending plan.

The time I have committed to do this will be:

Date:_____ Time:_____

In summary, Strategic Spending is vital as it helps you take charge of your life.

If you cannot do this personally, how will you ever be able to do it when you run a business?

Make the time to work through this plan with your spouse so that you have a joint sharing of these responsibilities.

Most people wait until they are in trouble before they start to do their 'budget'. Strategic Spending is about being proactive and planning ahead.

4 The Wealth Account

I have developed the concept of a wealth account - linked to the strategic spending system - which has worked successfully for my clients for over 20 years now. The idea of strategic spending is to divide your hard earned income up into small, easily controlled bundles. The first bundle taken out should be savings—a minimum ten per cent of your gross earnings. This amount is transferred monthly into your *Wealth Account*, which should be a Cash Management Trust or similar. If you leave savings till last, you will always find there is nothing left over.

The second bundle is your *Cash Account*. This covers your daily living expenses for which you normally pay cash; a bit like your pocket money. These are all non-deductible items. This account is simply accessed by a 24-hour access keycard.

The third bundle is your *Operations Account*. This is for those larger expenses which are usually paid monthly, quarterly or yearly by cheque. This account should not be linked to the Cash Account (i.e. you cannot access it with your Cash Account keycard). We keep the bundles separate. It is wise to use this account in conjunction with a credit card for those occasions when your monthly expenses are higher than the budgeted amount. The card acts as a smoother, as next month will be a surplus that can be paid back into the credit card.

In addition to your savings, which go into your Wealth Account, you should also put in enough funds to cover all your tax deductible expenses. This will save time and effort for your accountant when preparing tax returns.

The system is linked by the use of the *Transfer Account*, into which your pay is deposited. From there, periodic payments are set up to transfer funds to all the accounts on the 15th of each month. You should maintain a small float in the Cash Account and Operations Account.

The main aim is to accumulate as much as possible in the Wealth Account and use these funds wisely to create wealth.

You can use the example Wealth Account in Figure 2 to link up with your strategic spending plan. Once you have committed to strategic spending and keeping track of your spending using this system, you are well on the way to achieving your goal.

> **'Don't go around saying the world owes you a living. The world owes you nothing. It was here first.'**
> **Mark Twain**

To summarise:

- Set up your three separate accounts (your wealth system)
  Wealth Account
  Cash Account
  Operations Account
- Use your strategic spending sheets to track your monthly and yearly spending.
- Excellence is a commitment to completion
- There is no right or wrong; there is only outcome.
- Some people would rather be right than happy

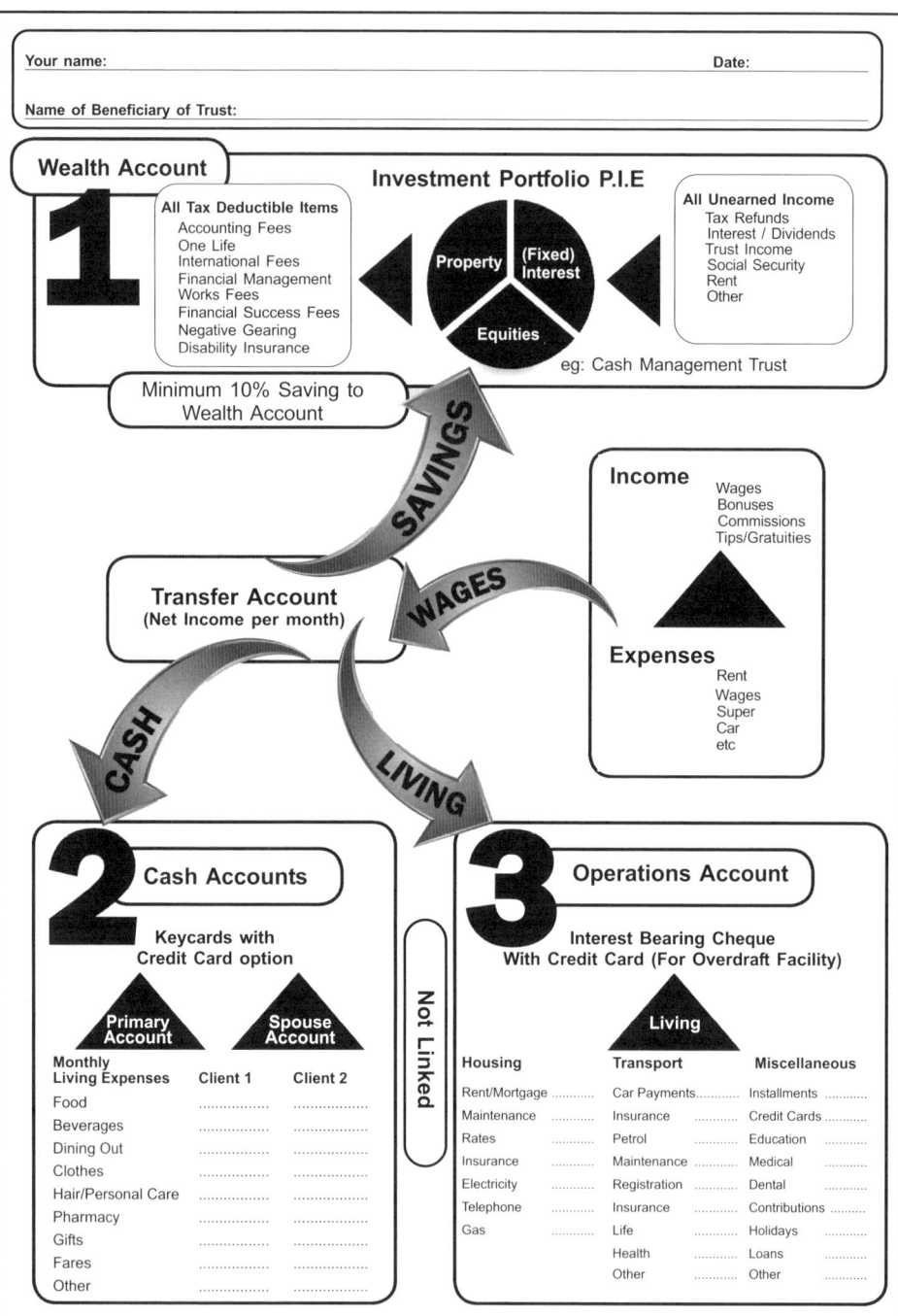

Figure 2

NOTES

Taxation

~

*'In this world nothing is certain
but death and taxes.'*

Benjamin Franklin

5 Taxation

I advise my clients that they have an absolute responsibility, legally, to pay what is due to the Tax Department. Never *evade* paying tax; however, you have the right to legally *minimise* your tax.

Always, and I do mean *always*, declare all income received, be it by way of cash or cheques, invoices, tips, gratuities—any form of remuneration of any kind that is legally assessable must be declared.

Please understand that I am not an accountant. I am a business person.

Over the years, I have discovered that tax is really an issue of common sense and there are extremely highly qualified people to give you advice.

You need to pay for the best advice you can get, because if you don't address these matters, you are making a contribution to the Tax Department of up to 48.5 per cent of the income you receive.

The greatest return that you can ever gain, consistently, and guaranteed from the government, is to minimise your tax.

For most people that could be a 30 to 48 per cent saving. That is a very hard yield to beat with an external investment.

In other words, by minimising your tax it's similar to investing and gaining a return of more than 30 per cent.

Therefore, the main avenue you have is in the area of minimisation. That is to say, claiming all deductions that you are rightfully entitled to claim.

A word of warning—Part 4 (a) of the Tax Act indicates that if your main intention to do something is basically to minimise your tax, this action may later be disallowed.

Most clients with reasonable incomes can claim between $5,000 and $10,000 worth of deductions; however, a lot of people have no idea that they are missing out on these.

For example, in the 1990's the Tax Department issued a statement to enable business people using a mobile phone, for the purpose of business, to claim a double tax deduction.

Yes, that's right; you could claim the mobile phone twice—as an individual PAYG and through a company.

This is a fairly simple process and all it requires is an understanding of the Tax Act to make the claim.

This also applies to laptop computers.

The Tax Act is like having approximately 25 telephone books of information. Hundreds of thousands of tax cases over the years have determined the Act.

In my seminars, I refer to the little thin book called a Tax Pack. The information we are going to talk about is not in that Tax Pack, which is designed to deal only with very basic deductions and how to fill in your tax return.

When the Tax Department writes to you, they address you as 'Dear Payer'. Does that give you a hint?

I bet when they write to James Packer, they don't say 'Dear Payer', they probably say 'Dear Mr Packer' or 'Dear Sir', or perhaps even 'Dear James'.

The laptop computer and the mobile phone represent thousands of dollars worth of deductions. Despite the fact that these have been available for many years, it is always such a shock to people - when raised at my seminars - that they aren't claiming them, or didn't even know they could.

In my seminars I ask, 'How many of you have worked back past 6 o'clock at night?'

Seventy to eighty per cent of the hands go up.

I then say, 'Keep your hand up if you claim that as a tax deduction.' All the hands go down. So I ask, 'Why didn't you claim it?' There are blank looks.

I then ask for those in the audience who have worked back past 6 o'clock for ten years or more, four nights a week. A number of hands go up.

I then say, 'I don't know whether it is applicable to you; however, it may well have been. You may have been able to claim for working back past 6 o'clock, say, $30 a week for ten years. That would be $30,000 worth of tax deductions. This may have represented approximately $14,000 back to you.'

I then ask those who have put their hands up, 'Would that be valuable to you?' Of course it would.

It may have been possible. There were awards that enabled you, if you were, say, a clerk and you worked back past 6 o'clock, to receive a meal voucher. This was tax free money in your hands. All it required was a request to your employer to pay you for that meal voucher and you would have received, say, $7 for the meal voucher after 6 o'clock. Multiply that by four nights and you have $28. Multiply that by 48 and it reduces your taxable income by $3,000 a year.

All you needed to know was that you could have claimed it. A lot of people are allowed to claim those sorts of deductions under their Awards.

An older woman in the group speaks up, 'Why don't they tell us these things?'

My response is, 'They are so busy. Did you ask the right question? Were you aware?'

Unfortunately, most people use a very ordinary tax group to do their return, thinking they don't have many deductions, or they get their mother-in-law to do it, or they complete it themselves. They end up paying tax which, in my view, with better advice they often wouldn't have paid.

An example would be the old provisional tax.

- § There are approximately 240 Tax Deductions available for individuals (P.A.Y.G.) tax payers.
- § And approximately 260 Tax Deductions available for companies

So there are over 500 possible tax deductions available. The question is - *How many are you currently claiming?*

Ref: Financial Management Works Pty Ltd

6   Provisional Tax

I am often amazed at my seminars when people tell me stories about paying provisional tax and the strain that it put on their affairs; the shock of dealing with not having known that this was a tax they had to pay. Had they known they could have planned for it.

Generally, the conversation goes something like this.

James turns up to see his accountant with a smile on his face. The accountant shows him a seat and they sit down and the accountant says, 'I have got your tax return ready. We have a small provisional tax problem.' At this point, there is some surprise on James' face. 'What is provisional tax?'

'Haven't I explained that to you before?' asks the accountant.

'No', says James.

'Oh', says the accountant. 'Let me explain. What's happened is that you have earned money in an unearned income situation—that is to say, not taxed at source. Not taxed in PAYG, or through the environment where the government can take its portion first.'

'Oh', says James. 'What does that mean?'

'Well, the government wants to tax you for last year's tax', says the accountant, 'plus next year's in advance, plus 8 per cent.'

'How much is that?' asks James.

'Well you have earned $30,000 by way of profit in that real estate transaction, and the tax on that is approximately $15,000, plus $15,000 for next year, plus 8 per cent increase, gives you over $30,000.'

'But that's all the money that I have earned', says James, 'and I have spent it on stock for my business.'

'That is unfortunate', says the accountant. 'However, if we don't pay this in the next 30 days, you will be penalised by 20 per cent, over $6,000, and the penalty is not tax deductible.'

At this point, James falls off the chair due to lack of oxygen in the blood to his brain.

You will note that most accountants now have defibrillators in their rooms to re-start the hearts of their clients who may experience a heart attack from such an experience.

In a lot of cases there was no need to pay provisional tax. It wasn't that the accountant was inaccurate in his assessment. He just failed to do other things that could have been done, possibly afterwards, to minimise the situation by restructuring and preparing the client in a much more tax effective way.

Because a lot of clients are able to minimise this tax issue and only a proportion of clients ever really paid provisional tax in advance, the government has subsequently removed this tax burden with the introduction of the GST. So, it's not an issue anymore.

However, all those who experienced the pain would understand the embarrassment and the difficulties that arose from the lack of knowledge and preparation for such an issue. In some cases, it caused bankruptcies.

I have had clients explain to me that they ended up getting divorced over the provisional tax issue.

What I am saying here is that preparation is everything in tax matters. Information helps you prepare to take the appropriate action so that you know exactly where you are, and you are not shocked into reactive mode in dealing with the issues.

Ninety-five per cent of the population deals with tax matters after the tax year is over.

We advise our clients to do a pro-forma tax return somewhere from March to April.

All this means is they guesstimate their position, deal with a tax adviser prior to the end of the tax year and work out, on the assumption of the last few months of income and expenditure, what they will actually face in terms of taxation.

This gives them time to plan and take appropriate action to minimise their obligations.

Real planning, however, should begin from 1 July and appropriate action should be taken throughout the whole year to minimise the amount of tax one has to pay.

In my seminars I get people to say and repeat after me three times, 'Tax is optional'.

I would like you to say this as you read this book, **'Tax is optional, tax is optional, tax is optional'**.

What does that mean?

The Tax Department gives you the option of arranging your affairs in a manner in which you pay only the tax that you are legally bound to pay. It is your option to minimise that tax by taking appropriate action—through structuring, through planning, through whatever is appropriate.

If you fail to take this option, then the Tax Department will merely take from you a percentage of all your earnings, and you will pay the appropriate tax.

So; it is your option and therefore, being optional, you can make a contribution if you so desire.

Begin with the end in mind and figure out precisely and accurately - and following good advice - what would be the appropriate tax you would like to contribute.

By taking this view, you feel you are actually a contributor and it is your option to contribute, just as you would to a charity.

In the olden days, there wasn't a Tax Department, there was the Church, and people contributed to the Church, and the Church looked after the parishioners.

Throughout the centuries, taxes have always been brought to bear on the rich; however, it was the poor who always paid.

The reason for the taxation was to help the community, just as the Church used to help the community. Unfortunately, it's a much more complex issue now and there is so much wastage.

My job is not to preach to you and tell you what you should and shouldn't do. All I know is that tax is optional and it is your choice whether you wish to take the option.

There are many, many deductions that people are not claiming. In my program and our support programs, I cover in some detail how to deal with what you need to have you make the correct contribution.

By way of example, below are some tax deductions you may wish to bring to the attention of your accountant to see if they are applicable to you:

- Salary sacrifice, such as superannuation
- Pre-payment of invoices
- Double deduction on mobile phones
- Double deduction on laptop computers
- Structuring income through a trust
- Being paid through a corporation
- Employing people through a corporation.

As a final thought, tax should not be an issue for your investment strategies. It should just be part of the puzzle. It is a jigsaw piece in the puzzle of financial freedom and it must be given appropriate time and expense to deal with it.

In Summary:
- 💲 Get the Best Advice You Can
- 💲 Take Appropriate Action
- 💲 Minimise your Contribution
- 💲 Remember—Tax is Optional!
- 💲 Spend Time with Your Accountant having them do a Proforma Return
- 💲 Saving Tax is Like Receiving a Cash Bonus from the Government

Leverage

~

*'Using borrowed capital for investment,
expecting profits made to be greater than
the interest payable.'*

**The New Shorter Oxford
English Dictionary**

7 Leverage

Leverage, for me, is using $1 and turning that $1 into $1 million in seven years.

I was explaining this at a seminar not long ago and a man at the back asked this question, 'Which is the best vehicle to create leverage with?'

'How long is a piece of string?' I responded. I went on to say, 'This is really not to be smart; however, it does have an answer that depends on who you are and what you want as an outcome.

'There are three main vehicles to use to achieve leverage,' I continued, 'first, Property; second, Equities; and third, Businesses through which you can use other peoples' time and other peoples' money.'

A young man at the front raised his hand and asked, 'Where did *you* start?'

'I started in real estate as it seemed to be the simplest process with the greatest leverage available.

'All that was required was to put a deposit down, borrow some money, the price went up and you made a profit.'

A lady in the middle row put her hand up and said, 'It sounds too easy.'

'Well, it *was* very simple', I said. 'However, those were the days of high inflation when all you had to do was put a pin in the Herald, and where the pin landed you bought and you made money.

'Today it takes more skill; however, there is a tremendous amount of opportunity in the real estate market to really win.'

An older man put his hand up and asked, 'And what did you do next?'

'I realised that money was simply made in real estate; however, you needed a cash flow to stay in the game.'

The young man in the front row said, 'So that is when you went into business.'

'That's right', I said. 'Cash flow is the blood supply and businesses give us that cash flow. For property transactions, there is a time lag between developments - and markets can change.

'I went into a real estate business. It continued to give me that cash flow while I learned more about how to trade real estate, which eventually led to developments and working with joint venture partners in real estate transactions.'

'So it's like working hand in glove', said the lady who asked the first question.

I answered, 'That is absolutely true'.

'Where I really gained tremendous knowledge and information was on leveraging shares through options and futures contracts.

'This was a tremendous leap of faith for me. As a property person and then a business person, I have to say, I wasn't anywhere near as secure in dealing in shares because they appeared not to be real to me.

> **What you focus on in life expands... so think about what you want!**

'I found in time that with the right advice, not being greedy, learning patience, using a system and a strategy, there are as many opportunities in the stock market as there are in the real estate market. And, in one sense, there is greater opportunity, as international share trading is made so simple with today's technology. It truly is a whole new world of opportunity'.

An older man in the seminar put his hand up and said, 'But doesn't leverage increase the risk, and haven't you a chance of losing all your money, even faster?'

'Absolutely', I responded. 'Leverage is a two-edged sword. It can increase your return and it can also increase your losses.'

You must be very careful in leveraging your position not to play with money that you cannot afford to lose—borrowed money is harder to pay back than your own cash.

It just means that, while the cash money is lost and you don't owe anything to anybody, the borrowed money can be lost and you still owe the money. Let's look at an example of this, so that we understand how leverage really works.

Let's take a simple example where you bought a home unit for $300,000 and, say, the home unit went up by ten per cent—you would make $30,000 (leaving out tax and fees etc).

Instead, you purchased this property with a twenty per cent deposit, $60,000, and you borrowed eighty per cent of the $300,000 being a $240,000 loan. Let's say the loan is at an interest rate of 7 per cent. Just multiply 7 x 240 to give you an annualised figure.

Let's say the rent equals the mortgage payment and includes the rates and taxes so we get a neutrally geared loan. In other words, no expenses - the rent equals the outgoings.

If the property goes up by ten per cent, as in the first example, then the value increases by $30,000. However, you have only $60,000 in equity terms (that is, cash in—disregarding legal costs for the moment) and your growth is $30,000.

The question would have to be asked, 'What return did you make on your $60,000 investment?' The answer is $30,000, which is a fifty per cent return, even though the property only went up by ten per cent. How did this happen? Leverage.

We must also look at the reverse of this.

Say the property lost ten per cent of its value.

In the first example, the property went down by $30,000 so you have lost ten per cent, assuming you bought the property for cash.

In the second example, the property went down by $30,000; however, you had $60,000 worth of equity in this property. As a proportional loss, you have lost fifty per cent of your equity.

You can see how leverage can be a two-edged sword. When the prices are going up the way you want them to, you win big time. However, when the price goes the other way, you can lose big time.

The leverage game is certainly the fast lane and it is designed to get you out of the rat race. It must, however, be engaged in with care and with thought.

In terms of a business, the leverage of that business is leverage of people working for you. It is about people who work so that you don't have to.

It's about small amounts of money working very hard through products and services, and basically, it's a game of leadership, marketing, positioning and strategies.

Once you get the recipe for this game you may well join the three per cent of the world's population who control ninety seven per cent of the world's money through businesses.

Interest is a leverage game with money and time. Rent is a leverage game with property and yield. Productivity is a leverage game of people's time, usually through systems and technology in business.

All of these are leverage games and all you need to know are the rules so you can play the game. All of my programs on property, business and shares are designed to teach people the rules of the game and how to win.

To summarise, at the end of the day it all comes down to these very important steps:

- Don't be Concerned with the Good Opinion of Others
- Don't get Attached to the Money or Things
- Be Willing to Give Up Control so You Can Play a Bigger Game
- Leverage is the Best Game in Town, If You Know the Rules.

> Remember, you do not use income to create assets.
> You use assets to create income.

NOTES

Yield

∼

'The amount of money brought in (eg interest from an investment, revenue from a tax); return.'

The New Shorter Oxford English Dictionary

8   Yield

Yield, or return, follows from the previous chapter of Leverage. It is through leverage that your yield or return is generally increased; as per the example of the cash purchase of the property as compared to the example in which eighty percent of the funds used to purchase were borrowed.

This shows one instance of a ten per cent yield against a fifty per cent yield when leverage is applied; and is just one of many techniques for increasing yield.

In the case of an option on a property, the yield can be extraordinary.

An option is a right, not an obligation, to control something.

I use options frequently in my business dealings and when trading in real estate.

An example of increasing yield, using an option, is a property I purchased at 168 Willoughby Road, Crows Nest. The purchase price was $4.08 million, with an option of $20,000 for six months.

In other words, I had control of a building worth $4.08 million for six months, with an option fee of $20,000.

Within three weeks of taking out the option on that building, I was offered $1 million for my option.

This building had the potential for adding another two floors. It was valued, with this potential, at $5.7million.

The person paying me the $1 million stood to gain an extra $700,000 worth of profit in the transaction, if he was to proceed to completion.

I wasn't particularly interested in selling, even for that substantial profit, as I wanted to use the building for my own needs. This example exemplifies what $20,000 can do, as far as a yield is concerned, in a very short period of time.

What sort of return is $1 million for $20,000 over three weeks?

Obviously, this is an exceptional yield that serves to demonstrate, once again, the potential leverage of an option and what can be achieved in a relatively short time.

There are many examples of yield that can be demonstrated here; the bottom line is that, as an investor, you must achieve consistently high yields to make your money work harder.

Alternatively, you will end up with lazy money; it is unfortunate to see lazy money in the hands of people who are not prepared to concentrate and focus on having their money work hard.

A five per cent yield with an inflation rate of three per cent means a real rate of return of two per cent.

This is like watching paint dry and will never support you to achieve real wealth unless you are dealing in hundreds of millions of dollars.

I believe that you should be looking for at least fifteen per cent return on your investments, if not twenty per cent.

For those who have relatively small amounts of money at work, particularly, it is reasonable to have your money working harder.

One of the success formulas that I use in our Abundance program is what I call the 90/10 strategy:

- Ninety per cent of the money you invest should be in a diverse portfolio - spreading the risk and minimising possible losses with the other ten per cent of your money made to work really hard.
- Using this strategy, an investor is prepared to take a greater risk as only 10 per cent of the portfolio is being risked if you break this up into small components.

In this formula, an investor is looking at returns of 100 to 1000 per cent and more, using options and other strategies that I cover in detail in our Abundance program.

As I explained the formula I use in our Abundance program, a man put his hand up at the back and yelled out, 'Aren't these risky things to do?'

'Yes', I answered. 'however, if you do this with small amounts and spread the risk with high yields, you can afford, on a 500 per cent return, to lose on four out of five transactions, and still be ahead of the game.'

In summary, the main strategy here is to use a very small amount of money to gain a very, very high yield.

9   Strategic Plan

As discussed in earlier chapters, having a Strategic Plan is extremely important on the journey of turning $1 into $1 million in seven years or less.

Fundamentally, there are three areas to invest in: property, fixed interest securities and equities.

This spells P.I.E.—Property, Interest, Equities.

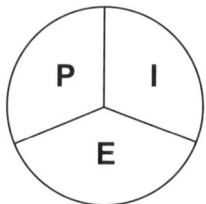

Figure 3

What does your PIE look like? Some 95-percenters have a PIE like this.

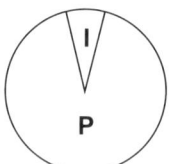

Figure 3a

They are paying off a house and have a small amount of money in the bank. Not a very balanced portfolio.

As previously mentioned, property represents an extremely important part of the portfolio. The area of equity, however, is equally as important.

Equity can sometimes be a little confusing as the term encompasses a number of different interpretations.

The New Shorter Oxford English Dictionary defines equity as: '1) Fairness, impartiality, 2) The value of a mortgaged property after deducting charges and claims against it, 3) The issued share capital of a company (also equity capital); the shareholders' interest in a company.'

We would like to look at the third meaning - equity representing shares, which includes shares in companies. A shareholding in a company you own is, in fact, a direct equity investment.

Managed funds, in the general sense, comprise equities or properties, which are managed by a Fund Manager through a trust. These are generally listed.

This enables an investor to put small amounts of money into a very large diversified portfolio.

From a strategic point of view we are talking about the creation of a spread or diverse portfolio using property, fixed interest securities, equities, and business, including trading opportunities.

A formula for success is to understand the above and then create a strategy to implement the diverse portfolio.

As discussed previously, one of the success formulas that I use is to take ten per cent of the portfolio and put it to work, really hard, by taking the greater risk of using it for trading.

For example, if you had a $100,000 portfolio of shares in what is termed a "buy and hold" position - i.e. you have invested on a relatively long-term basis in a diversified spread portfolio - you then take ten per cent of that portfolio and actively trade it.

This means that you keep ninety per cent of your portfolio in a moderate to volatile environment (the longer the term the more controlled this would be) and taking ten per cent of that portfolio, actively trade it to create a higher yield.

> 'A man of knowledge lives by acting, not thinking about acting.'
> Carlos Casteneda

I cover trading opportunities in equities in the next chapter.

In summary, the success formula indicated here is:

- Leave Ninety Per Cent of Your Portfolio in a Diversified Spread
- Trade the Remaining Ten Per Cent with the Expectation of Achieving More than 100-1000 Per Cent Yield Per Year on At Least Part of This.
- Transfer Proportional Amounts of the Profit From the Trading Position to Your Buy And Hold Position, Creating Long-Term Wealth.

NOTES

10 Momentum Trading for Success

In terms of equities, what you are looking for are companies that have been managed profitably, long-term.

What you are really buying is the future management and the yield - or dividend - which would come from the buy and hold formula with shares, producing a capital gain.

Another way to build wealth, and particularly in the short term, is to use the strategy of momentum trading.

The 'buy and hold' strategy tends to be based on fundamentals whereas the momentum trading process is technical trading, short term—a highly leveraged process.

I am a property person and have been for 40 plus years now. Equities were always a bit of a mystery to me; I therefore sought the expertise of the very best.

When looking for advice, choose the best and pay for it, as I believe your investment will be well made in the long term (if you pay peanuts you get monkeys).

I met a man named Dr Claus Gerling, a German who married an Australian and settled in Australia. His doctorate is in finance and, in my mind, he is a genius.

The thing that really impressed me about Dr Claus is he is a full-time trader himself and he acts for other companies. He has advised banks and stockbrokers, so he has to 'walk his talk'.

He doesn't just theorise on the aspects of trading, he is also a Licensed Commodity Trading Adviser (Australian Financial Services Licence No. 218770) and is audited by a number of government and industry groups.

When I first met Dr Claus I asked him if he could show me how to be successful at trading shares. His answer was, 'Of course.' In his German accent he said, 'All you need is to be disciplined and not to be impatient or greedy.'

'For me that would be difficult', I said.

He smiled and said, 'That is very true. Ninety-five per cent of the population is impatient, greedy and undisciplined.'

He went on to say, 'The most important part of trading is that you become conscious of these ingredients and you are emotionally fit to handle the losses that come with trading shares, options and futures.'

He then went on to explain that ninety five per cent of the population knows how to make money if shares go up and asked, 'Would you like to know the secret formula?'

'Of course', I said with anticipation of some miraculous piece of advice from this master of share trading.

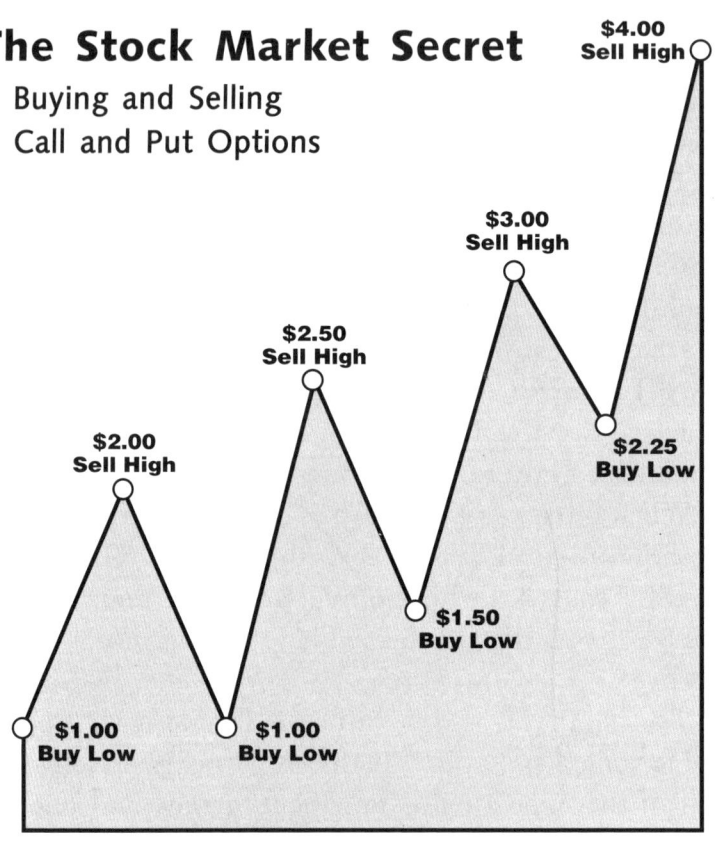

Figure 4

He then drew a graph (see Figure 4) and said, 'You can buy a share for $1 and it may rise to $2 and then fall back to $1 and then rise to $2.50, go down to $1.50 then rise to $3, go to $2 and go on to $4, and so on'.

I said, 'I have seen those graphs and they look a bit scary.'

'Not if you know the secret formula', he said with a smile.

'What is the secret formula?' I asked, being really impatient.

'**You buy low** and **you sell high**', he said with a smile.

'I am paying you $40,000 a day for this?' He nodded and said, 'Of course. You buy the share for $1, you sell it for $2 and you make a dollar.'

'I understand that', I said most disrespectfully.

'What percentage of the population knows how to make money when the stock market falls?' he said with a smile on his face.

'I didn't know you could make money when the stock market falls', I said with a new hope of some secret being shared.

'Would you like to know the secret formula?' he asked. 'Absolutely', I replied.

'You sell high and you buy low', he answered with a smile on his face. 'You sell for $2 and you buy back for $1.'

'Is that legal?' I asked.

Dr Claus replied, 'Of course, banks do it every day. This is called "shorting". An even smarter strategy than this is to buy a "put" option.

I had no idea what a 'put' was as this was the first time I had ever heard the expression.

'You mean to say you can sell something that you don't own?'

'Absolutely', Dr Claus replied, 'and the interesting thing is, the market takes a long time to build its confidence up, then when it falls, it generally falls quickly. Often more money is made in falls than in rises'.

With a smile on my face, I asked, 'Are you expecting a crash?'

Dr Claus hesitated, smiled and said, 'Yes, and we can hardly wait.'

I went on to say, 'So you mean you can make money when the stock market rises, and you can make money when it falls, and when it falls you can often make more money?'

'Absolutely', Dr Claus said in his careful, precise Germanic way.

'That is amazing!' I exclaimed. 'I didn't know you could do that'.

In my seminars I ask the question 'Who has heard of puts?' and generally about twenty–thirty per cent of the audience puts up their hands. I am always amazed that they know about this and I didn't.

'I then ask, 'Who actually trades them?' Only a few hands are raised.

Knowing something and doing something about it can be miles apart.

A put is extremely important when you have a share portfolio.

For instance, you may have a long-term buy and hold position (e.g. your superannuation fund) and know the share, generally, has been going up. You also know, however, the company is going through hard times and is going to get some adverse publicity. You don't really want to realise the share's profit at this point - and pay tax and brokerage on that realisation - because, in the long term, you think the share will recover. You also don't want to miss out on the falls.

By using the 'put option' you have an opportunity to trade the share down, separately, without cashing in your long term position.

Dr Claus put another question to me: 'How would you like to get a loan for $175,000, no questions asked with a $2,000 exposure?'

'That would be fantastic', I said, waiting for his explanation.

How do you get a $175,000 loan with $2,000 of your own money with no credit requirements and no questions asked such as, 'Where do you live? If you have lived there less than 3 years, where did you live previously? Where do you work? If you haven't worked at that position for 3 years, where did you work previously?'

Dr Claus went on to say, 'National Australia Bank is a very good share. Back in 1991 you could have bought it for $6 and today it's over $30.

'Let's say you wish to buy 5,000 National Bank shares at, say, $35 a share. You would need approximately $175,000 to acquire 5,000 National Bank shares.

'Assuming the shares went up by $1, you would make $5,000 on your $175,000 investment. What sort of a return would that be?' Dr Claus asked me.

'Two point eight six per cent', I replied. (Maths was one of my better subjects at school).

'That is right, and so many people are so excited when they get 2.86 per cent return on $175,000. You know how many people have $175,000 lying around in a shoe box', he said with a mischievous look.

'We could buy an option on National Bank shares for perhaps 40 cents or $1.00. An option is a right, not an obligation to control something. It's a premium to buy time.

'There are sellers out there with shares who will give you an option which is a premium for a certain time to access their shares.

'Control is more important than ownership', he went on to make a point of principle.

'You mean I can take an option on shares for a small fee such as 40 cents and, in so doing, control a share portfolio as if I owned it?' I said.

'Absolutely. You would spend 5,000 times 40 cents, or $2,000, plus a small brokerage, and this would in fact give you control of $175,000 worth of shares for a period of time.'

I was astounded at the simplicity of the statement and the magnitude of the possibilities.

Being a property person, I would give options on property. I never understood that you could use them on shares. I also never realised the extent to which that could open up possibilities.

Let's say you took 5,000 options at 40 cents which would cost $2,000 and the share went up from $35 to $36, making $1 profit. If the option had a Delta of one, the option would go up $1 as well.

If you had 5,000 options increasing in value by $1, you would make $5,000, less a small brokerage.

'$5,000 profit on a $2,000 option, what sort of a return is that?' he asked.

I thought for a few seconds and I could hardly speak to announce the fact that it was 250 per cent return.

And this could be achieved in a week, two weeks, three weeks. 'What sort of a return would that be?'

'Astronomical'. I replied, enthusiastically.

He went on to explain, 'It's a massive leverage game when there is a two-edged sword.

'If you let the trend be your friend and follow the herd you will be amazed how often you get this right. An excellent trader will get seventy per cent of his trades right and thirty per cent will be losses. The important thing is knowing when to take from it and when to exit the position.'

'Would you show me?'

'Of course', he responded, without hesitation.

I remember going home that night, being overwhelmed by the possibilities, and I could hardly wait to explain this to my son, Harrison. I now had another string to my bow to create an income stream that could really give leverage to his life, and to mine.

That was over eight years ago, and I have seen Dr Claus help people make substantial sums of money. I have also seen losses created by people becoming greedy and holding onto trades that they should have sold, not following the rules that Dr Claus has so strongly stood for.

Dr Claus runs *Momentum Trading for Success* every month for people who have never traded before.

He teaches paper trading programs with a mythical $10,000 bank, or five $2,000 lots, so there is no risk of capital while you learn how to trade.

He recommends spending five minutes to half an hour every day, looking at the options section of the newspaper and/or on your computer, to maybe take five or six positions a month.

Every couple of months at Dr Claus' program he runs a competition to determine who will be the best trader in the weeks following the program.

The prize is a book; inevitably a woman wins it because she follows the rules. Women know how to make a cake; they follow the recipe!

Some of the men have been known to make a greater yield than the women, but in general, they don't follow the recipe and therefore don't win the prize. I hope you think about this; It's a great lesson for all.

This leads me to the next step, *Trading for Profits*.

11 Trading for Profits

Dr Claus runs an advanced live trading program which covers both cfds (contracts for difference, options and futures.

There are over $43 trillion traded every day on world stock and currency markets and these shares, options and futures are traded with a key stroke. In so doing, you access a world of finance the potential of which is beyond most people's comprehension.

Trading for profits is a 12 month home study program designed to support participants in making the transition from paper trading to live trading. The program consists of a 2 day live trading seminar on dvd with monthly follow up workshops, 12 months of access to the trading pro trading site along with 12 months email support.

On the trading pro site participants have the opportunity to see which trades Dr Claus is making on a daily basis, the positions he is selling - or dumping - and new positions he has taken.

Trading has such opportunities; if you are greedy and impatient, however, you can lose a lot.

It's a game of psychology - eighty percent psychology, ten per cent skill, ten per cent knowledge.

My strongest recommendation is that you paper trade for at least three months before you invest any money, and then only a modest amount. Never invest money that you cannot afford to lose and, overall, hasten slowly.

To Summarise:
- Follow the Recipe
- Don't get Emotionally Involved
- Cut Your Losses
- Let Your Profits Run, and, Have an Exit Price with a Profit Target
- Don't Be Too Greedy
- Don't Invest in the Market any Amount That You Cannot Afford to Lose
- Don't Try and Second Guess the Market—it has Power Greater Than You, and it is Fickle
- Be a Trend Follower, Not a Speculator.

12   The Six Masteries

It's no good just thinking about it, you've actually got to change the habits to which you are accustomed in order to bring balance to your life.

The various areas of your life can be grouped under the following six masteries.

These masteries are a system; they are a system of life, and your financial success is a by-product of the system you currently have in action.

If money is not flying into your life, it is due to the way you have set up your system.

If you have tried many times before and failed, I believe my program will work for you if you follow my recipe; if you surrender to it and are willing to be coached. You will need a different attitude, perhaps; you'll need to use the strategies and follow specific plans and techniques. You will definitely need to take action.

The following is the basis behind my personal success.

The Six Masteries are:
No. 1 - State Mastery

This is your emotional state; your positive actions; who you are being; your consistency and enthusiasm in your life tasks. When you are out of *state* you are not empowered. You are not focused and your outcomes are usually ineffective.

No. 2 - Money and Career Mastery

Money gives us choices in life, and while it is not the most important thing, without money we are very limited. If you do not have money handled, it will always cause you concern. It will limit your actions.

Similarly, your career development is a source for your income and self-fulfilment, both commercially and emotionally.

No. 3 - Relationships Mastery

Your relationships with your spouse, co-workers, neighbours and clients are about communication and who you are. The quality of your communication determines the quality of your outcomes in life. The possible richness from relationships often can be the most important issue to people in their lives.

When you get sick and tired of being sick and tired, you'll change.

No. 4 - Health Mastery

Your vitality, your well-being, your fitness and energy; everything about your day-to-day activities is limited if you are in poor health. If you became rich, but are sick all the time, would you call that success?

No.5 - Time Mastery

The ability to warp time; to work smarter not harder, to get more out of life and to have things balanced in your family, your work, your money, your health—all the aspects essential to living a harmonious life.

No. 6 - Spirit Mastery

I am talking about universal consciousness. Spirit and religion can be miles apart. You can be spiritual and religious. You can also be religious and not spiritual or spiritual and not religious.

> 'Money is a living entity, and it responds to energy exactly the same way you do. It is drawn to those who welcome it, those who respect it.'
> Suze Orman

I am clear that there is a power greater than who we are "that doeth the work." We can tap into this awesome power, like we would tap into our state. We can tap into infinite possibilities. Ultimately, all wealth creation is guided by natural laws. On this planet we co-create.

A special note with this book:

I strongly recommend that you take what you like and leave what you don't.

Bob Proctor has a very simple definition of education. He says "An educated man is one who can entertain himself". Secondly, an educated person is one who can entertain somebody else. Thirdly, an educated person is one who can entertain a new idea.

As you read this book you will be challenged with more and more new ideas that will perhaps disturb you—perhaps press buttons which will be based on beliefs that, generally, were not yours to start with, but were passed on from others.

I am responsible for my life, for my feelings and every result that I get.

Bob Proctor

I know I am a spiritual being, living in a physical body having a human experience; that is intelligent. I have a creative spirit ... my humanness gives me my fears.

Roy McDonald

The Million Dollar Session

∽

'Render more service than that for which you are paid and you will soon be paid for more than you render. The law of "Increasing Returns" takes care of this.'

Napoleon Hill

13 The Million Dollar Session

How could one session be worth $1 million? **You could be a millionaire?** Is that really possible? ABSOLUTELY, and I'll prove it to you.

Firstly, from the book *The Instant Millionaire*, the author, Mark Fisher, asked 'How do some people earn ten times more money in their lifetime than the rest of us? Do they work ten times harder? Are they ten times smarter?' Of course not! They have a system—a very simple system.

Money is a game. It is a very important game and you need to know the rules. If you know the rules, and follow them, you'll win. If you don't know the rules you'll lose. There are many secrets to these rules. Can you learn them? Yes, absolutely!

Most people make a million dollars in their lifetime, many people make a lot more. If you earn $25,000 a year for 40 years, $1 million will go through your hands.

Most people, in fact ninety five per cent, will have almost nothing left when they hit 65 years of age.

Where do we learn about money? Generally, we learn mostly from our parents, and of course you need to consider whether they were really successful. *Were they great examples with their money or were they a warning?*

Do you remember when the Commonwealth Bank man came to the school and gave you a little yellow moneybox? Whatever happened to those little moneyboxes?

When we fail to learn a lesson, we get to take it again...and again! Once we have learned the lesson, we move on to the next one. (And we never run out of lessons!)

Money is such an important subject, yet it is not at all important if it is working for you. It's like sex. Money and sex are the hottest subjects. If they are working there's no problem, if they are not, they're a major issue.

A large number of all divorces result from disagreements about money.

Understanding money, how to make it, how to grow it, how to keep it safe, is absolutely essential to your life—essential to your relationships, your happiness and, ultimately, your future.

Let's look at the statistics on what an Australian family is up to, financially, in this money game.

According to the Australian Bureau of Statistics, approximately twenty five per cent of families in this country live under the poverty line: that is, they earn less than $15,000 per year. More than eighty per cent of families earn less than $60,000 per year. Only one per cent earns more than $120,000 per year. As an individual you have a five per cent chance of earning more than $60,000 per year and less than one per cent of earning more than $120,000 per year.

14 Twelve Secrets of Wealth

I will share with you my policies, which I call the twelve secrets of wealth.

Wealth Secret No.1
Watch Whichever Way the Crowd is Going and Go in the Opposite Direction

Ninety five per cent of the population aged 65 are dead, dead broke, or on the pension, so why would you want to go where most other people go?

It will be difficult because you will be going against what most people are doing and you will be out of the ordinary and therefore, perhaps, isolated.

But I can assure you of more friends in the long run—real friends who will admire you for your courage.

Wealth Secret No. 2
Look for Problems, as They are Often Opportunities in Disguise

Often, in real estate terms, it's finding things that people don't see, or seeing the property in a different manner—creating something different.

In a gold mine, if you look for dirt you find dirt; however, if you look for gold...

Wealth Secret No. 3
Understand Values

Knowing how to value things is very important. Until you know value, everything is worthless. It is not about price, it's about value.

It's about buying below the average market price and selling above. In real estate terms, there is an average market price and property is either sold 10–30 per cent below that average price, or 10–30 per cent above that average price, depending on the motivation of the seller or buyer.

Wealth Secret No. 4
Money is Just an Idea

In fact, money is a complete illusion. People often confuse value with cost. It's a common assumption that if you pay a lot, it must be worth a lot.

Money and value are often in the eyes of the beholder. Money can be easily created with positive action, as well as easily lost with negative action. So if you put money in its proper perspective, it's just a tool. Something that you can create from the position you take in life.

Money always flows to great opportunities. Money is always attracted to great ideas.

What do you think is the most important—to have a lot of money, or to have a great idea? The idea is always the most important, in fact it will attract the money necessary to have the idea work if the idea is good enough.

Wealth Secret No. 5
He Who Lives by the Golden Rule Gets the Gold
Integrity and honesty will pay off in the long run, and you'll get to keep the money.

Wealth Secret No. 6
Be Prepared to Take Risks and Face your Fears
There is no shortage of opportunities in Australia; or the world, for that matter. There is, however, a shortage of courage.

In all the fairytales; if you want to marry the princess, you have to slay the dragon. Your greatest dragon will be facing your own fears.

> 'The greatest mistake you can make in life is to be continually fearing you will make one.'
> Elbert Hubbard

A common fear, which is necessary to face, is borrowing money to invest. You will be asked to face this fear many times as you move out of your comfort zone.

Wealth Secret No. 7
Attitude Problems are Greater than Money Problems
In other words, you must have the strong, positive attitude of wanting to be wealthy. You must love a challenge, you must be goal orientated and you must consider obstacles and barriers as just temporary inconveniences.

Wealth Secret No. 8
Accept Failure as a Learning Experience
If you are not failing, you are not trying hard enough. It's like skiing down a mountain—if you are not falling over, you are not extending yourself.

"Successfully wealthy people always have failures, they also always have more successes than failures.

Unsuccessful people not only have few failures, they also have few successes because they don't do very much. They tend to stay in their comfort zone; tiptoeing through life, hoping they'll make it safely to death - and end up on the pension anyway.

> 'It's a funny thing, life. If you refuse to accept anything but the best, you very often get it.'
> W. Somerset Maugham

Wealth Secret No. 9
You Have Abundance in Your Life and You Have all that You Need to Acquire Absolute Success
It all depends on just one specific aspect of your life, and that is, who are you going to become to have this work for you?

It is the 'becoming' of a successful financial person that leads to the ultimate outcome of success.

Wealth Secret No. 10
How is Your Networking? Using Your Network Will Save You Leg Work
You need people you respect, coaches and advisers, in all

areas around you—including an excellent tax accountant, lawyer, planner and financial adviser to do your financial engineering.

Ultimately, you must take responsibility. Whilst they are accountable to you - in the end *you* make all your decisions.

Wealth Secret No. 11
Invest For the Long Term
Getting wealthy is a long-term business and a lifestyle, not a 'get-rich-quick' scheme.

Take a position, hold that position, choose it carefully. Once chosen, take a long time to change your mind.

Wealth Secret No. 12
Become Consistent in Your Process of Being Disciplined in Acquiring Assets and Actively Managing Them
Consistent routines bring results 99 out of 100 times. An average person with a modest routine of daily self-improvement will outperform a disorganised genius.

You don't have to be a genius, you just need to be consistent.

Bonus Wealth Secret:
Be Open to New Ideas and Have Diversification as Your Form of Success
Eighty per cent of all growth comes from the selection of the right portfolio mix. So, make sure that you understand the investment strategies and the investment products.

You don't necessarily have to be an expert, although you have to at least be able to explain it to somebody else and, particularly, yourself.

If you do not fully understand what you are doing, either don't proceed or have a very small exposure while you learn whether or not this is a worthwhile venture. Ultimately, as discussed before, there are only three areas to invest in:

1. Property (P)
2. Fixed Interest Securities (I)
3. Equities (E).

Everything on the planet is one or a combination of these three investments.

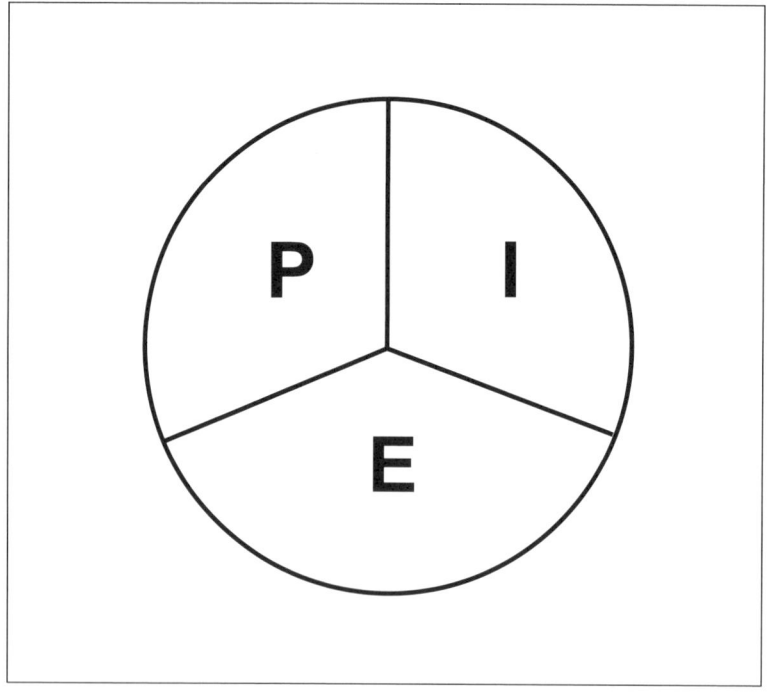

Figure 3

NOTES

Twelve Wealth Strategies

~

What does being wealthy mean to you?

15 What Does Being Wealthy Mean to You?

| Income | $_____? |
| Assets | $_____? |

Ninety five per cent of the population **can't define what wealth is.**

It's about **cash available** and **current debts**—95-percenters have no idea and don't really want to know.

How much are you **currently saving per month** and what is your **tax position**? How much **do you owe** and what are your **prospects**? These are very basic questions (see figure 5).

You have to **lock it in**—95-percenters make it a moving target, like a cake of soap in the bath.

You have to make it **realistic and attainable**—95-percenters go for $100 million when they are earning $40,000 per year.

You must **get started**—95-percenters never start because they think they will never be able to achieve it.

Wealth for you must be a *must*—95-percenters make it a *should*.

You must have **a plan**—95-percenters just wander around bumping into things.

You must put your plan into **action**—95-percenters just talk about it.

You must make yourself totally responsible for your money - 95 percenters give responsibility of looking after their money to the others.

Never give up—95-percenters fail because they give up early.

You must run your life like a **business** and each year you must make a **profit**—95-percenters run their lives into bankruptcy.

You must **focus on your outcome**—95-percenters worry about what others say, think or do.

You must seek out **quality advice**. Pay for the best you can—95-percenters usually ask family or friends. These people, generally aren't going anywhere.

Benchmarks give you a **Quick Look** at where you are and where you want to go:

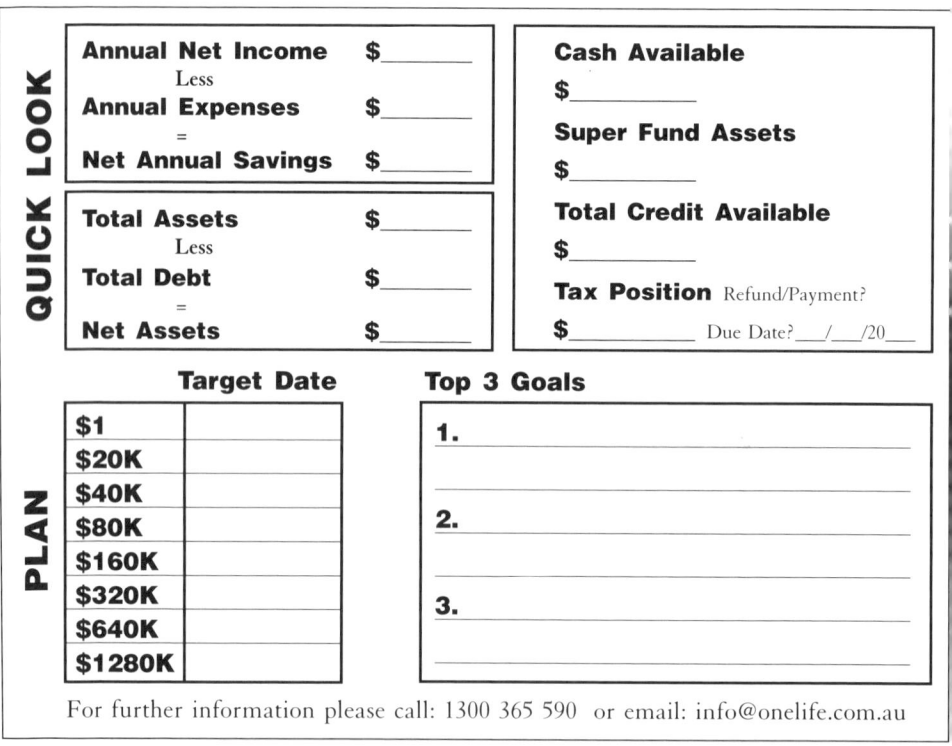

Figure 5

Let's look at the twelve strategies for becoming wealthy.

16 The First Wealth Strategy: Value Each Dollar

Value each dollar that flows into your life. A simple dollar coin may not look like much, but it is a seed.

Like an acorn, this seed will grow into a money tree. If you just care for it, plant it wisely and look after it, it will grow and produce millions of other seeds.

Wealthy people think of a dollar just like that. Poor people think of it as a small piece of metal which you can spend very quickly, and which doesn't buy much.

Let's look at some statistics. With a $1 coin, if you invest it in a bank account with say 3–5 per cent interest, it's going to take a long, long time to become $1 million. At 3 per cent it will take 468 years.

Let's see what happens if you plant some more seeds. For example, $1 per day ($30 per month) at 3 per cent growth will take 147 years to make $1 million.

If we raised the interest rate from 3 per cent to 5 per cent it cuts it down to about 100 years, but that's still not fast enough, is it?

At 10 per cent interest, your dollars will grow into $1 million in 56 years. Now that's a bit more interesting.

In other words, $1 a day could grow into $1 million in the span of a normal lifetime.

Let's see some comparisons with other alternatives. If, since the day you were born, your mum and dad put aside $1 every day until you retired at 65 years of age and had invested it, at 15 percent per annum you would have $50 million by the time you retired.

You won't believe this, but if this same $1 per day had been invested at 20 percent per annum compounded, at 65 years of age you would have more than $1 billion—that's one thousand million all from $1 per day.

So you can see why a simple $1 coin might not appear to be very valuable; invested correctly over a long period of time, however, it can make an amazing difference.

To understand this fully, you need to understand the power of *compound interest* and *time*. Einstein himself said, 'The most powerful invention of man is compound interest.'

Compound interest is a money magnet. It works while you sleep; it works 24 hours a day, 7 days a week, 365 days a year. All you need to be is consistent.

Now, let's look at a great example of this.

17 The Magic Game of Golf

'The Effect of Compounding'

In my seminars I ask, 'Do we have any golfers here?' A few people raise their hands. 'Let's say you are playing a game of golf where you bet 10c on hole #1 and compound the bet at each hole up to hole #36. How much do you think you would bet on the last hole if you played to 36 holes?' I ask.

A young man calls out from the back of the room, '$36.'

'More like $360', says a middle-aged man. Then a young woman raises her hand, 'I think it would be about $1800.'

'They are all good guesses. Let's see how this works with 18 holes.'

Hole 1 — .10c	Hole 10 — $51.20
Hole 2 — .20c	Hole 11 — $102.40
Hole 3 — .40c	Hole 12 — $204.80
Hole 4 — .80c	Hole 13 — $409.60
Hole 5 — $1.60	Hole 14 — $819.20
Hole 6 — $3.20	Hole 15 — $1638.40
Hole 7 — $6.40	Hole 16 — $3276.80
Hole 8 — $12.80	Hole 17 — $6553.60
Hole 9 — $25.60	Hole 18 — $13107.20

'That's pretty amazing. So, how much do you think you would bet on the **36th** hole? Would you believe that the answer is more than **$3.4** billion?' The room is quiet while they try to digest what I have said. 'I found that the most staggering number. Imagine if somebody had actually agreed to play and you were really good!'

So, you can see from this example the importance of compound interest and how hard your money is working for you with very little effort on your part. To repeat Einstein's words; compound rate of return is the most powerful invention of man!

You don't have to be a genius, you don't have to own a big company; you can do it from home. You can be financially independent.

Let's get started. Suppose you could put away $200 per month, and set your target to grow at 20 per cent per annum for the next 20 years.

Now, I know you might think that 20 per cent is difficult; however, with carefully selected stocks and real estate, or a small business on the side and a properly geared position, you may be able to do this.

Saving $200 per month at 20 per cent for 20 years grows into $632,000. Now that's good.

Instead of starting now, just say you waited for one year. In other words, you only have 19 years. The last year will cost you $116,000.

In other words, procrastination is a very expensive process.

If you extended from 20 years to 30 years and held off one year late from starting, at $200 per month it would cost $842,000 for waiting just one extra year—almost $1 million. That's over $2,000 a day, or $100 an hour.

The most important principle to get here is what I call the 'tenth multiple'.

It is extremely important to understand how slowly this money grows, yet it takes as much time for $1,000 to become $2,000 as it does for $500,000 to become $1 million.

The most important process for wealth strategies:
- You must *start* the saving process
- You must *keep it up* (weekly/monthly)
- You *watch it* very closely
- You *actively* manage it.

Tip 1—The Tenth Multiple

The tenth multiple demonstrates the exponential growth of your money. The effect of doubling demonstrates that $1000 will generate $1.024 million by doubling the initial sum tenfold. This system shows the dramatic increase in value during the last three periods.

Tip 2—Conversions

Annual to weekly

A simple way of calculating an annual sum to an approximate weekly sum is to take the first digit of the annual number and multiply by 2.

> 'Success is not to be pursued; it is to be attracted by the person you become.'
> Jim Rohn

eg $20,000 per year
2 x 2 = 4
= approximately $400 per week

Weekly to annual
In order to convert weekly sum into an approximate annual sum, divide the first digit of the weekly amount by 2.

eg $300 per week
3 ÷ 2 = 1.5
= approximately $15,000 per year

Tip 3 —Rule of 72

An easy way to express how long it will take to double your money, based on a compound interest rate, is to divide a factor of 72 by the interest rate.

eg 72 ÷ 20 per cent = 3.6 years (say 3.5 years approx.)
      72 ÷ 15 per cent = 4.9 years (say 5 years approx.)
      72 ÷ 10 per cent = 7.2 years (say 7 years approx.)
      72 ÷ 6 per cent = 12 years

(see figure 6)

Let us see what effect that would have on a single investment of $2,000 - made today by a 25 year old - by the time they reached age 63, at 6 per cent, 10 per cent, 15 per cent and 20 per cent compound rate of return.

Year Factor (72) - $2,000 invested in 2008 at age 25 years

@	FACTOR	2008	2009	2010	2011	2012	2013	2014	2015	2016	2017
6%	12	$2,000									
10%	7	$2,000							$4K		
15%	5	$2,000					$4K				
20%	3.5	$2,000				$4K			$8K		

@		2018	2019	2020	2021	2022	2023	2024	2025	2026	2027
6%	12			$4K							
10%	7					$8K					
15%	5	$8K					$16K				
20%	3.5		$16K			$32K				$64K	

@		2028	2029	2030	2031	2032	2033	2034	2035	2036	2037
6%	12										
10%	7		$16K							$32K	
15%	5	$32K					$64K				
20%	3.5		$128K			$256K				$512K	

@		2038	2039	2040	2041	2042	2043	2044	2045	2046	2047
6%	12							$16K			$19K
10%	7						$64K				
15%	5	$64K					$128K				
20%	3.5		$1024K				$2048K				$4096K

Would you prefer $19K (6% compound) or over $4Million (20% compound) in your superfund?

Figure 6

Dollar Cost Averaging

How much you invest is not as important as how consistently you invest the same amount over a long period of time. This is called dollar cost averaging.

This is particularly relevant in times such as these when we have seen the markets fluctuate somewhat. It works like this—if you save a fixed sum each month into a unit-linked accumulation program, the average price paid over the period is less than the average price per unit. Here is an example of how it works.

Month	Unit Price	Amount Invested	Units Bought
1	$1.00	$100.00	100
2	$2.00	$100.00	50
3	$1.25	$100.00	80
4	$1.00	$100.00	100
Totals:	$5.25	$400.00	330

The average price of units over the four month period is **$1.31 ($5.25 ÷ 4)**, but the average price paid is only **$1.21 ($400 ÷ 330)**.

The more the unit price fluctuates and the longer you invest, the more you benefit from this principle.

Conclusion: Uncertain times are not necessarily bad times.

Remember, you can be a millionaire with as little as $1 a day.

18 The Second Wealth Strategy: Actively Manage Each Dollar

The Rockefeller family had wonderful teachers and they were taught the following rules. They were to divide their income to cover the following areas.

1. 10 per cent of what they received had to be given to the church, in other words, tithed.
2. The next 10 per cent was to pay themselves, to save.
3. The next 10 per cent was for their taxes (depending on the tax bracket, this could be anything from 0 per cent to 30 per cent of gross income).
4. Mortgage payments or rent.
5. Household expenses, eg food, clothing, television etc.
6. Transport costs, such as car payments, fuel, repairs, registration or public transport fares.

7. Fun and entertainment costs, such as movies, holidays and dining out.
8. Insurance—health insurance, life insurance, home insurance and so on, including superannuation.
9. Miscellaneous expenses, including debt.
10. Business expenditure.

Those ten categories are broad and simple, easy to arrange and easy to understand.

Millionaires consider their money just like this. They control what they are doing, they know what their expenditure is, they take time to consider income and expenditure and as they get busier they have people to look after that for them.

Here is a seven step formula millionaires use in handling their expenditure.

1. They plan for needs and procrastinate for wants.

2. They shop for value.

3. They ask and expect discounts for every purchase they make.

4. They examine their receipts and accounts.

5. They categorise their receipts (they put them in a 1 to 10 category) as per the Strategic Spending sheets.

6. They balance their accounts, whether it be cash, credit cards or cheques.

7. They file their receipts when they get home—they have a system.

Filing receipts is a very important area. Some of the receipts have tax deductibility, which is a great reason for filing them.

If you can get a tax deduction for an expense that you are legally entitled to (in the 47 per cent tax bracket) then that is an instant 47 per cent guaranteed return on your money from the government. That's a hard return to beat, anywhere, so fast.

It may surprise you, that through my research working with very successful individuals that I commonly find that the taxes very wealthy people pay are anything from 4 per cent to 10 per cent annually, with an average of about 6 per cent or 7 per cent tax.

These positions are taken through careful planning, good advice and understanding the rules.

These things are only important if you are serious about being financially independent.

19 Other Wealth Strategies

The Third Wealth Strategy - Make Money
There are only two ways to make money: work for it; have it work for you.

It is important to have at least five forms of income. One of those income forms is from your own work. Most other forms of income will come from leverage, either through investments or through business.

Making money must always be regarded as the 'river of gold'—the cashflow, the life force which drives your financial destiny.

Remember that making money is different from investing money, as investing can be passive (eg in a bank). Making money has an entrepreneurial side, so it is important that you are actively managing your investments.

The Fourth Wealth Strategy - Save it
Wealthy people love to save money, they like to buy wholesale and rarely pay retail.

They have a Wealth Account for accumulation and they save consistently.

The Fifth Wealth Strategy - Invest Wisely

Wealthy people learn how to invest their savings at millionaire rates. Anyone can invest their money at three per cent or four per cent. How do you grow it at ten per cent or twenty per cent?

This is usually achieved through gearing and getting a better yield on your money through active, not passive, management.

You really need to be a conservative investor, a moderate risk investor and a volatile risk investor. You need a combination of the three risk levels, which have been carefully selected based on your own special risk profile.

You need to be a long term investor, which will lower your risk.

This is not a 'get-rich-quick' scheme, this is a 'get-wealthy-slowly-and-keep-it' game. Don't play the market on short term exercises. This is very dangerous, particularly in the stock market.

Note the distinction of option trading, which is a trading game for income. Not a 'buy and hold' game, which is designed for long term growth.

The Sixth Wealth Strategy - Financial Protection

Protect your money through trusts and good decision making. More on this later.

The Seventh Wealth Strategy - Spend Strategically

Spending strategically is an essential part of your wealth creation strategy. This is not about budgeting. It is about having abundance awareness, and choosing in which areas you will spend your money.

The Eighth Wealth Strategy - Become Tax Effective

The tax department should be your friend, not your enemy. You really need to familiarise yourself with all the opportunities that are available to you to minimise your tax, legally.

The Ninth Wealth Strategy - Know Your Risk Profile

It's important to take on investment strategies with ease and grace. You need to know your risk profile, with the area of exposure where you are still comfortable. There is no point making investments which make you wake up screaming in the night, because that's only going to give you more stress.

There is a simple test which will determine what sort of investor you are; the risks you are prepared to take for the rewards you intend to gain. It is essential to know exactly where you stand.

- $ How do you currently track your spending patterns?
- $ What steps are you taking to legally minimise your tax?
- $ What risk profile would you generally have:

In the table below the example shown is of a relatively high risk taker. In the blank spaces put the percentages you feel comfortable with.

	Conservative	Medium	Volatile	
eg	10%	60%	30%	= 100%
	__%	__%	__%	= 100%

The Tenth Wealth Strategy - Use Leverage/Gearing

Leverage/gearing is a vital element in increasing your yield and accelerating the process of wealth creation. Leverage is the tool that all strong investors use to gain higher yields or return on their capital.

It needs to be very carefully used because leverage/gearing is a two edged sword. You can increase your return providing you've got growth; however, if the investment falls in value the gearing works exactly the same way, in reverse, and you can lose a substantially higher proportion or all of your capital invested.

So it must be done with precision and in a balanced way. It must also be understood that gearing will change a conservative or moderate investment to a more volatile investment because of the borrowings which have been placed on that investment.

The Eleventh Wealth Strategy - Share It

Share your money with your family, enjoy your money with your friends. Remember that you are only a temporary steward of the money—it's all the Great Spirit's anyway.

You arrived on the planet wrinkly, with no hair, no teeth, and no money, and you may well leave the planet the same way!

The Twelfth Wealth Strategy - Plan, Plan, Plan

All wealth secrets are important; however, the single most important wealth creator is planning.

There is an old adage which says, 'It wasn't that you planned to fail, but you failed to plan'. It is so important just to take time out as you are, now, to really consider these issues and then put them into action.

I believe that you must have twelve month, three year and five year plans, supported by monthly and quarterly reviews.

My experience has led me to the conclusion that the reason most people don't plan is not because they haven't got the time to, it's that they don't know where they are going.

What happens is that they go into what I call 'drift mode'. This is a very dangerous situation, as they have given up a certain part of control over their future and are not taking personal responsibility.

Twelve Wealth Strategies:
In summary, the twelve wealth strategies are:
1. Make sure you value your money
2. Make sure you actively manage your money to increase your yield
3. Have cash flow from five forms of income.
4. Make sure you create a wealth account and save a minimum 10 per cent of everything you earn
5. Invest your money carefully and with precision
6. Protect your money through diversification, insurance, trusts and other techniques
7. Spend strategically
8. Become tax effective
9. Know your risk profile
10. Use leverage/gearing to enhance your yield
11. Share your money with your family and enjoy it
12. Plan, plan, plan.

Bonus: Make sure you take action

20 Twelve False Wealth Assumptions

We all have to deal with many wealth myths. These are false assumptions which are based on incorrect information and some have been around for a long time. They have almost become cliches.

They are just myths, similar to how once upon a time people thought the earth was flat. They also thought the sun revolved around the earth.

If you build your financial house on shaky foundations, it won't stand the test of time.

No 1. Real Estate Prices Always Go Up

That is just not true. Take the Sydney residential market in December 1988. Over approximately the following 24 months, the real estate values in Sydney dropped by more than twenty per cent in some areas and struggled to recapture the position for the next seven years.

No 2. 'Position' is the most important element in real estate

This is not always true. An example of this is when a Real Estate Agent sold property at Seven Hills, renamed it Kings Langley by putting a covenant on the site and they doubled the price of the land.

They said 'position, position, position', everyone believed them and they made a fortune.

You will often pay a premium for position and therefore the yield has to be massively increased to offset it. Often the premium could be far in excess of the value.

No. 3 Having a Good Secure Job will Lead You to Wealth

There is no security in a job—ever—only security in yourself. Unless you add value you won't have a job in the long run.

In the 1700s, ninety per cent of people worked for themselves on farms and as merchants or manufacturers of some kind. By the early 1900s, only twenty per cent worked for themselves.

In the 1970s, only six per cent actually had their own business or were what we would call 'entrepreneurs'. It was over ten per cent in 1996.

The world is still changing and the whole social and economic fabric of our planet has shifted. My belief is that people will become more independent and interdependent, working for themselves as we go further into the 21st Century.

No. 4 Saving Money is a Good Investment

There are only two places to invest your money.
1. Invest in something that is really growing (and that's not in a savings account)—the only way to make money in a bank is to own the bank.
2. Invest in yourself.

Saving money is never an investment. Saving is a temporary parking place to accumulate money to invest in growth-orientated investments which you actively manage.

People whose wealth strategy is to deposit money with others only do so because they do not know how to invest. Basically, they don't know what they are doing so they have 'passive investments' which are savings account-type investments. They give the money to somebody else to make money with their money, and after taxation and inflation they usually lose capital.

Winston Churchill once said, 'Saving is a fine thing, especially when your parents have done it for you.'

Saving is, however important. As noted above it is a very important step in the wealth building process.

No. 5 All Debt is Bad

Like most statements, there is usually a little bit of truth in these things; however, it depends what debt we are talking about. Consumer debt is extremely bad. Tax deductible and investment debt can be extremely valuable, and in fact you can't build real wealth within a realistically short time without it.

Good debt, is debt that is Tax Deductible and the investment is growing

No. 6 It is Bad to Fail

Without failures you would not have grown and learned anything. Indeed, failure is a very important part of success. You must develop a very positive mental attitude about failure as you can learn so much from it.

With every failure there is an accompanying lesson. Just remember the golden rule, with every door that closes another door opens. It is unfortunate that most people focus on the door that closes, not the one that is open to them.

No. 7 Wealth is Measured by How Much Money You Have

Money is only the appearance of wealth. It is not the substance, it is only the form. Wealth is not about things, it is about thoughts and actions. You must think wealthy and act wealthy. You can have a lot of money, in fact you can be rich, and not be wealthy at all. Wealth is a state of mind, it is an attitude.

Being broke is a temporary inconvenience, but being poor is a mental disorder.

You could pick any successful person, take all their money away, and within five years they would probably have it all back again.

No. 8 Security is the Most Important Thing

It is unfortunate that our country has such an obsession with security—job security, social security, superannuation security.

Security is only an illusion. There is only one place where security lives and that is between your ears. It is the same place where recessions come from.

Security is driven by fear, and the converse of fear is faith. So you must have faith in yourself.

No. 9 The Government / My Employer is Responsible for My Well-Being

There is only one person responsible for your financial well-being, and that is you—and you must take absolute responsibility.

It is important to note the difference between responsibility and accountability. For example, your accountant is accountable to you, and you are responsible. You are 'at cause'.

So many people give away control and responsibility to others in their financial affairs and finally come to the shock realisation that things weren't handled properly.

No. 10 To Acquire Wealth, Someone has to Lose and You must Win

That is not always true. Often, wealth is created best when two or more people win. There is an infinite source of wealth and abundance on this planet, all you need to do is tap into it. In my seminar I show, step by step, a real estate transaction in which everybody wins.

No. 11 You Need Money to Make Money

What is more important is a good idea. If you notice how really wealthy people operate, they very rarely use their own money at any time; in fact they are constantly protecting it and using other people's money.

One of the most important areas in wealth creation is to operate like a wealthy person does - having a wealthy mindset. To become wealthy, the quickest thing you can do is to act like a wealthy person and create a wealthy self-image.

You then have made a major step in what I would call 'the becoming' of a wealthy person. All you really need to do is do what wealthy people do.

In my seminars we do an exercise about a $100,000 inheritance. I ask what participants would do to invest that money. We look at bonds, shares in the stock market, gold, reducing debt, putting the money in the bank, buying a new car, giving to charity, going into business, investing in property trusts, buying real estate, and giving to the family.

I have been asking this question as an exercise for the last 10 years and I am always amazed by what people would do. In the surveys that I have done, I have asked them to invest $100,000 over ten years with the objective of doubling it to $200,000.

How many people do you think could do that? These are ordinary people who have been given the money to plan a portfolio. Do you think the figure would be ten per cent, twenty per cent or perhaps even thirty per cent? Would it surprise you to discover that only one per cent could actually double their money in 10 years? To a large extent that's fairly poor, even just to double it. There were no millionaires, and forty per cent weren't even able to hang onto the original $100,000.

My understanding of why this happens is that people don't understand the basic principles of wealth creation.

No. 12 As a P.A.Y.G.* You Can't Get Many Tax Deductions

P.A.Y.G.s have tremendous opportunities for tax deductions. In fact, as I have impressed upon you earlier in this book, in this country tax is optional. It has been for many, many years. It is your option to take action to legally minimise your Tax.

This is always a surprise to people, as I believe there is a kind of robotic mindset of the salt-mining type; salaried workers who feel they just don't have any choice in the matter.

As an example, negative gearing could provide a tax deduction for one's entire salary.

Obviously, you'd have to consider whether this is a wise way to go, given there are tremendous tax breaks in the lower income areas (eg no tax on your first $6,000).

For instance, if you declare a gross taxable income of $20,000, your tax is just over $2,000, which is less than

* Pay As You Go

fifteen per cent of your income (similar to living in Hong Kong, or your superannuation tax).

This area is a very acceptable tax threshold to be in.

Most tax deductions are driven by income levels which are generally in excess of $80,000, where taxation tends to amount to a substantial rate (40 per cent for every dollar above $80,001 effective from 1st of July 08).

To summarise, the twelve false wealth assumptions are:

1. Real estate prices always go up.
2. 'Position' is the most important element in real estate.
3. Having a good secure job will lead you to wealth.
4. Saving money is a good investment.
5. All debt is bad.
6. It is bad to fail.
7. Wealth is measured by how much money you have.
8. Security is the most important thing.

> 'Whatever you can do, or dream you can,… begin it. Boldness has genius, power and magic in it.'
> Goethe

9. The government / my employer is responsible for my well-being.

10. To acquire wealth, someone has to lose and you must win.

11. You need money to make money.

12. As a P.A.Y.G. you can't get many tax deductions.

21 The Billion Dollar Success Plan

You must **crystallise your thinking**—build the image. Determine what you specifically want to achieve.

Being in a powerful resourceful state is everything. Creating a strategy in this state guarantees your outcome.

Now **dedicate yourself** to its attainment with unswerving singleness of purpose.

Develop a plan for achieving your goal and a deadline for its attainment. Use your **seven year plan**, then your yearly plan, monthly plan, daily plan, hour by hour. Read your goals daily.

Develop a **sincere desire** for the things you want in life. A burning desire is the greatest motivator of every human action. You become **conscious** of what you are seeking, and you **create success habits**.

Turn it over to Spirit (let go and let God)—you have the greatest power in the Universe working with you on this project.

Develop a **supreme self-confidence in yourself** and your abilities. Proceed with all activities without the possibility of failure.

Concentrate on your strengths, manage your weaknesses and **focus on your outcome.**

Develop a **determination** to follow through on your plan, regardless of obstacles, criticism, circumstances or what other people may say, think or do.

Expect with all your heart and soul that Spirit will reward you openly for your **faith.** Expectation is one of the most powerful forces in the Universe, as it will guide you and create **focus, attention** and **intention.**

> 'Successful people do what unsuccessful people won't.'
> Jim Rohn

Know **you are your greatest asset.** Invest in yourself at least ten per cent of your income - in education and knowledge.

Create the best possible **environment** at home and work for yourself, to be on purpose and to contribute.

The game you can't win—you can only play.

If you don't have enough money in your life there is one primary reason—**you have not conditioned yourself for wealth.**

You may have WWI
No, not World War I.
You have Wealth Wounds.

WWI	Associating negative things with excessive money.
WWII	Too young.
WWIII	Too old.
WWIV	Not smart enough.
WWV	Not enough time.
WWVI	No money.
WWVII	No credit rating.
WWVIII	Don't know how to invest.

Story Story Story

Don't imagine what it would be like to be wealthy—imagine what it would be like to live after you have become wealthy.

If you believe these stories you will be right. If you don't believe them, you will also be right

You can never get beyond certainty—you have to start beyond it.

The **greatest secret to investing** is **asset allocation** and **compounding rate of return**.

The **greatest secret to wealth** is gratitude. If you can be grateful for what you have, you are wealthy. If you do not have gratitude in your life, no matter what you have, you are poor indeed.

The **secret to freedom** is to
Enjoy Your Life,
Master Your Money, and
Live with Passion.

NOTES

Debt free in five years—financially independent in a further seven years

∼

'The reason so many individuals fail to achieve their goals in life is that they never really set them in the first place.'

Denis Waitley

22 Debt Free in Five Years

Debt free in five years - financially independent in a further seven years

Ten years ago I was the key speaker at a seminar. A man came up and said to me, 'You can't be debt free in 5 years if you own a home'.

I said, 'Really, do you mind if I use you as an example?'
'This will be interesting', he responded.
'Can you save 10% of your gross income?' I asked.
His response was 'If it means I will be debt free in 5 years, absolutely'.

The following table shows the solution to this man's and his wife's financial position.

Clients	Gross	Tax (Approx)	Net	Spending & Saved
His Income	$55,000	$17,000	$38,000	$2,400 Fixed
Her Income	$35,000	$ 8,000	$27,000	$1,000 Cash
				$1,200 Other Services
Total	$90,000	$25,000	$65,000	$750 Saved
Per Month	$ 7,500	-	$ 5,400	$5,350

Save 10 per cent $750 per month

	Major Debt $	Monthly Payment $	Interest Rate	(Factor)	Payment Ranking
House	100,000	1100	10.5%	90	5th
Car	20,000	450	15%	44	4th
Grace Bros	2,000	350	21%	5.7	2nd
Bankcard	1,300	300	19%	4.3	1st
Personal loan	4,500	200	23%	22.5	3rd
Total	127,800	2,400			

How do they repay the debt without any risk or additional expenditure?

	Repayment Progression	Debt Clearance
Bankcard	$1,300 repaid at ($750+$300)=$1,050 pm	1.5 mths
Grace Bros	$2,200 repaid at ($1,050+$350)=$1,400 pm	1.5 mths
Personal loan	$4,500 repaid at ($1,400+$200)=$1,600 pm	3 mths
Car loan	$20,000 repaid at ($1,600+$450)=$2,050 pm	10 mths
House loan	$100,000 repaid at ($2,050+$1,100)=$3,150 pm	32 mths
	TOTAL	48 mths

$3,000 pm = $36,000 compound @ 10% $2,200,000 over 20 years

Financially Independent in Seven Years

In order to demonstrate the following table, it is useful to develop an illustration which will allow you to simulate your own personal financial situation.

John and Mary own a house (valued at $350,000) which is entirely debt free. They have calculated that their living expenses amount to $25,000 p.a.

John's income:	$55,000	
John's tax liability:		($18,351)
Mary's income:	$35,000	
Mary's tax liability:		($8,941)
Total Income:	$90,000	
Total tax liability:		($27,292)
John and Mary's total net income:	$62,708	

In order for both John and Mary to become financially independent, it is necessary to build a capital base which is substantial enough to cover their expenses and is suitable for their lifestyle.

One of the options which John and Mary could take is to build a portfolio sufficient enough to allow them an annual income of $25,000.

In order to achieve this, John and Mary could build a negatively-geared portfolio around a capital base of $300,000.

The interest payments which John and Mary will be making are $30,000 p.a.

Because this is a negatively geared portfolio, the repayments will be offset against the income generated from the investment portfolio. This could negate the tax which would otherwise be payable on the interest received from the investments.

The base of $300,000 could grow (over a period of around seven years) at approximately 12 per cent to $663,204. After seven years, John and Mary repay the loan, leaving them with $363,204.

The $363,204 that has accrued from the last seven year's investment is now rolled over into a growth and income tax effective diversified investment portfolio which may return 12 per cent or $43,584 pa.

Mary and John split this investment income:
John's investment income: $21,792
Mary's investment income: $21,792

23 Ten Commandments for Creating a 'Financial Fortress'

1. Thou shalt avoid 'conspicuous consumption'.
2. Thou shalt avoid putting assets in thy own name.
3. Thou shalt never act as guarantor for anyone else's loan.
4. Thou shalt carry adequate liability insurance.
5. Thou shalt not serve on a board of directors.
6. Thou shalt avoid all personal debt.
7. Thou shalt operate thy business from a corporate entity as trustee.
8. Thou shalt not go into business without a detailed business plan / marketing plan / management plan.
9. Thou shalt never enter into a partnership without a partnership agreement, which includes the breaking up of the partnership.
10. Thou shalt never put all thy eggs in one basket.

Bonus: Thou shalt always assume the worst.
You were probably being optimistic. You have to plan for the worst and expect the best.

24 Preservation and Protection of Your Wealth

You have a one in four chance, if you earn more than $60,000 per year, of being sued this year.

That's fairly high and is getting higher. There are a lot of people out there looking to gain from your position.

If you are a person with no assets and you are driving your car, which is unregistered and uninsured, it's not a big deal if you run into someone else's Mercedes Benz. You just get out of your car and say 'sue me'. If you've not got anything, it really doesn't make much difference.

If you are wealthy and you do anything wrong, on the other hand, you could lose everything.

One of the best arrangements that you can make to protect your wealth is to have it in a trust.

It would be recommended, if your intention is to be wealthy, for you to have an *asset trust* for all your assets that grow, and secondly to have a *trading trust* for your business.

With these trusts, ownership is not in your name but in the trustee's name, and you can become the beneficiary of the trust. In effect, you have control without the direct exposure that would happen in normal circumstances.

The secret to smart money is to live like a millionaire but be a pauper on paper.

There is a need for specialised advice here. As a graduate of The OneLife Abundance program you can access the Financial Management Works team by emailing admin@fmw.com.au

25 Eight Principles of Wealth

1. Choose Investments that are Powerful and Stable.
By powerful I mean that they can grow at high rates of return; by stable, that they will grow steadily, surely and relentlessly upwards in value without massive fluctuations.

Unfortunately, a lot of investments don't have these features together.

For instance, you would probably like to have investments that are very liquid - with no management headaches - and that you can borrow against; that are a hedge against inflation, good tax shelters, portable, have stable growth and generate steady cash flow.

Let me tell you, there is no such investment that can do all those at once. There is no 'right' investment. However, it is possible to have a combination, and a portfolio will give you these attributes. What you are looking for is stability and power.

Fixed interest securities often are stable and safe but they have no power. They can't produce the rate of return we are looking for. Commodities, on the other hand, are very powerful; in fact, they can produce spectacular results - and they often can produce spectacular losses.

Real estate can often have power and be stable. And it is not always perfect as it is not always liquid. We have got to know when to buy as well as what to buy and, more importantly, how to buy.

Stocks and shares, equities generally, have potential for great power. They can be used for leverage and they do have liquidity. And to some degree you can give up stability with this leverage tool as there are, frequently, fluctuations in the market, so there are risks.

If you look at the general return over the last 20 years from property, equities and fixed interest securities, pick any seven year combination and work out what are the best investments for the highest yield in Australia, you will come up with equities as the most powerful and stable investment over that time. You might, therefore, conclude that you should have 100 per cent invested in that area to give you the greatest return.

2. Always Consider Taxation and Inflation as Part of the Decision to Make Any Money.

If you don't take these two into consideration, you could get a real surprise about the outcome that you will ultimately receive.

3. Make Maximum use of the Assets You have.

Make all dollars work hard—don't have lazy dollars and don't have lazy assets.

Wealthy people buy very well and cautiously. They tend to buy quality, keep things a long time and look after them. They tend to pay cash for consumer items and don't put them on credit.

People who want to look like they are wealthy tend to lease expensive cars and boats and pay a very large premium to do so. The only borrowing wealthy people do is to make money on investments.

4. Diversify your Investment Portfolio, but don't Diversify Too Much.

I know that's a bit of a quirky statement; however, if you diversify and diversify and diversify you will get a very average return, because you have actually reduced risk at the cost of any real yield.

Eighty per cent of all yield is determined by knowing which markets to go into, so concentration is very important. This is not to say that buying direct investments and putting all your eggs in one basket is the answer but, whichever basket they are in, you do need to watch your eggs very closely.

People who have no idea what they are doing diversify endlessly. It's a bit like they are in a horse race and bet on every horse in the race and hope to win.

You can never win that way. It would be a much better plan to follow the next wealth principle in dealing with this.

5. Break your Investment Portfolio into Three Basic Categories:
- **Conservative**
- **Medium risk**
- **Volatile.**

Work out the percentages in each category and use them as your criteria for diversification.

Obviously, if you are older and getting closer to retirement, you are going to have less money in your volatile area and much more in the conservative.

If you are younger and you are building your wealth, you will tend to have more in the medium to volatile percentage, with little in the conservative area (only a small amount which we call 'fall-back money').

6. Your Money Must Multiply at High Rates of Return.

If you have $5,000 today and you want to turn it into $1 million in 25 years, you would have to have an average return of twenty four per cent after taxes and inflation.

If your goal was to do it in 10 years, you would need a return of forty per cent, fifty per cent or sixty per cent to actually achieve this.

These returns look impossible except if you use a magic formula. Most people have used it and not even known they've done it, and that's by using leverage; you can get smart investments to yield you in excess of 100 per cent return on your money.

Gearing like this is a two edged sword—the risks can go either way; you can also lose 100 per cent of your money.

7. It is Pointless to be a Defensive Wealth Creator, you Must be Offensive.

> **'No one can cheat you out of ultimate success but yourselves.'**
> **Ralph Waldo Emerson**

If you are so concerned about security, facing risks, failure or death, so-called 'safe' investments bring no yield at all. In a game of chess, the best defence is to attack. It is therefore important to be assertive, in fact even aggressive in your investment strategies.

This is not to say be foolish and do things without careful consideration.

Once you have determined a plan then *commit to that plan.*

Your exposure should always be such that you won't lose everything on one investment. By careful planning, you can *spread your risk* in such a way as to minimise the down side - even if you chose very badly.

Whatever you choose, look for *strong yield,* otherwise there is no point in making the investment.

8. Pay for the Advice that You Need to Get and Go to the Person who will give You the Best Advice.

It may cost you a little more however you will find, if the

person is skilled, it will be well worth it. As a test, advice should yield you at least five times its cost, for example, in taxation matters or investment advice areas.

Remember, James Packer doesn't use ITP to do his tax return. They can't afford to give you really smart advice, as their costing doesn't allow them to produce the outcome that you really need.

In summary, the eight wealth principles are:
- **Choose investments that are powerful and stable.**
- **Always consider taxation and inflation as part of the decision to make any money.**
- **Make maximum use of the assets you have.**
- **Diversify your investment portfolio, but don't diversify too much.**
- **Break your investment portfolio into three basic categories: conservative, medium risk, and volatile.**
- **Your money must multiply at high rates of return.**
- **It is pointless to be a defensive wealth creator, you must be offensive.**
- **Pay for the advice that you need to get and go to the person who will give you the best advice.**

Bonus principles:
- You should never, ever give up control of your money.
- What you focus on grows; what you don't care about or look at is soon lost.

26 Five Secrets of Running your Own Business

There is an important secret to growing wealthy; ultimately you must have either your own business, or an arrangement which enables you to own your own business within a company; so as to gain incentives and bonuses equivalent to owning your own business.

1. You Must be Passionate About What You are Doing.
My studies of all successful people in business have shown that they love what they are doing and they are not just doing it for the money.

If you are just doing it for the money, it is almost impossible in the long run to be successful, because the money will never fulfill your real desires and needs.

2. You Must Have Talent; You Must be an Expert; You Must be Special at what you do.
If you cannot be, then you must get someone who is, and promote them. You must be different and have a way of packaging what you do that makes it (and you) stand out.

3. You have to have a sense that what you are doing is your destiny.

In other words, you were born to do this. You are 'on purpose' in what you are doing.

These three secrets combine to form an absolute success formula. If you study successful people - and, particularly, the really wealthy ones who are consistent - they all have these three elements present.

4. The Reason to be in Business is to Give you More Life - Not to Give Your Life to the Business.

Most people give their life to their business. Most people get trapped in the business—having no time to spend with their family. Being in business should give you more choice, not less.

5. Acquire Your own Building.

One of the purposes of running a business is for the business to acquire a Real Estate investment. Your business should provide you with the income to acquire your own building to operate from.

It costs generally about the same to rent what you can buy, so why not own it, rather than pay someone else. In this way, you receive the capital gain and the improvements that you add to it are yours. And there is a feeling of confidence about, and commitment to, the future.

> 'We all have two choices: we can make a living or we can design a life.'
> Jim Rohn

My experience shows that, in asset terms, most businesses appear to make more money in the long run from the increasing value of the building they have purchased than the entire business has made from its capital growth.

In other words, the business provides an income flow whereas the building provides a growing asset.

Over the long term (if you are experiencing hard times, or if you have been able to reduce your ultimate debt on the building) you can determine the rent you really want to pay. As a tenant, you don't have that option.

Bonus Secret

Always Remember, Businesses Never Fail—People just Give Up.
It's like relationships, they never fail—people just give up and say they've had enough.

This may well be appropriate at the time, or it may be way too soon. I have seen people come to me with businesses that I believed had very little chance of succeeding, yet through the determination and commitment of the people they turned them around.

I have also seen people with businesses which I felt would be very easy to fix; however, the business basically fell apart because the people gave up.

27 Own Your Business

This is the most important thing - financially speaking - you will ever do in your whole life, and is the only way to real financial freedom. It is one of the five forms of income.

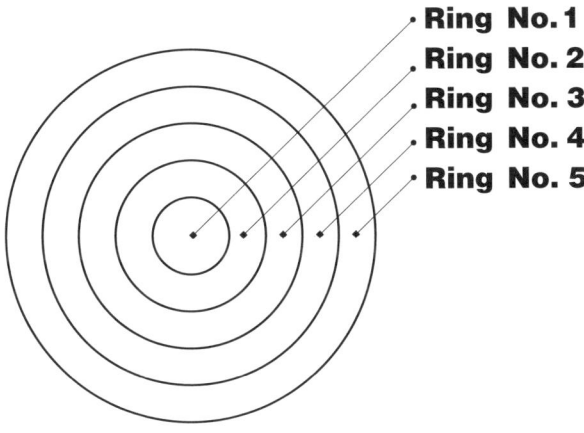

Figure 7

Ring 1: Core Expertise.
This is something that you are good at, something you know a lot about. You may have a new technology or may use old expertise with a new marketing strategy.

You are looking for a hungry market that wants to know what you know. You are looking for people who want to know that information. They are highly motivated to solve a problem or a frustration, and you have the answers.

Let's use the example of a school of fish, and ask the following questions.

- Does the market contain enough fish?
- Is the school of fish growing or declining?
- Where are the fish and what are their feeding patterns? Are they really hungry?
- Are the weather conditions ideal for fishing?
- Is there a particular bait that makes them bite like crazy?
- Are they willing to come out from the safe, dark depths and chase your bait?
- Have you got a process to land these fish, once they are on your hook, and bring them in?
- There is a special code which is required to process this whole marketing exercise. Cracking the code is where the secrets really lie.

Ring 2: Teaching Others how to Succeed at your Core Expertise.

Using real estate as an example, my job would be to train others to purchase real estate well.

You can come up with many ways of teaching people how to do things; via one-to-one information, processing through seminar training, classroom training, tele seminars, internet based trainings, books, magazine articles, mail, CDs, and DVDs.

Remember, if you are not good at these things it doesn't matter. You can have other people do them for you. If the idea is good enough, it can be processed by people with that expertise.

Ring 3: Teach these same Success Skills to Other People so that they can Sell to Other Clients.

In other words, replace yourself in Ring No. 2.

Ring 4: The Next Area is the Database.

It is essential that you create, and make good use of, a database which contains all of the clients that you have been building.

As well as helping you with running your own business, there are a number of other opportunities for these clients that either follow your business or someone else's.

This is often known as the 'back end' of the sale. So many people work to make a sale initially, with the real objective being the back end.

Other people miss this entirely, simply by not knowing. Apart from a mailing rental agency or a lead generation from other business, you could become a joint venture partner. You could also become a direct marketer to your own database.

Ring 5: You could Support Services for Other People in the Other Four Rings.

This is taking into consideration that you have learned how to work the four rings successfully, and that you could show others how to put their businesses into the same position.

This gives you great leverage; the systems that you have developed could now be passed on and franchised to many people.

Rules for Starting your Own Business

1. Know what business you are in.
2. Get 'on purpose'—do what you love and the money will flow to you.
3. Design your lifestyle, then choose the business that supports that lifestyle.
4. Become very good in your field of activity.
5. Ride the trend that is growing, instead of the one that is fading.
6. Be a copycat. You don't have to be the first in anything, you don't have to start the trend. You can follow others who are doing well in an area, but be different and improve it.
7. Watch your costs and overheads, particularly with employees. Be slow to hire and fast to fire.

8. Invest in the best technology you can afford, and in the training and development of your team.
9. Empower the team that you are working with and share your abundance with them. It is better to have three people earning lots of money and really going for it, than ten people struggling to make ends meet.
10. Know your strengths and weaknesses. Build on your strengths and manage your weaknesses.
11. Have around you the best team of advisers you can find. Your areas of weakness should be supported by people who are excellent in their roles (these people don't have to be employed, they can be on contract with a given end result and paid on an outcome basis).
12. Systems are the solution. Remember, you must allocate a minimum of 20 per cent of your time to work **IN** your business, and 80 per cent to work **ON** your business.

28 Five Magic Steps to Achieving Your Goals

There are five magic steps which you must follow to link your goals, intention, and purpose, with the power to realise them. That power lives within you and through alignment you can achieve anything you set your mind to.

1. Know Exactly Where you are Right Now.

> 'You can't rise unless you set goals that make you stretch.'
> Tom Hopkins

That is, where you are financially? To achieve this, you will have to do a realistic bottom-line statement: this is what I have in cash/assets; this is what I owe; this is how much my income is.

This is an essential process, and most people think they can skip this point and not worry about it.

You must take an inventory of your values and your internal strengths and weaknesses. You must increase your strengths and manage your weaknesses. You must gather around you people who can take care of the things that you are not so good at—a coach or mentor or accountant—whoever it is you need to have around you to have you be successful.

2. You Must Focus Upon a Specific Intention.

Intentions are very much a step up from goals as goals are often fuelled by fear.

People tend to do things based on fear, but with intention you do things based on careful consideration, and there is a sense of purpose about what you are up to. So with clear intentions, clear goals and plans follow.

3. You Must Have a Specific Game Plan to Deliver Your Intentions.

This is a step-by-step process. For instance, you could have an intention to be a millionaire in seven years.

> 'Most folks are about as happy as they make up their minds to be.'
> Abraham Lincoln

Your specific game plan will give you a program where you spend six hours a week for the next six months learning and studying through seminars, workshops, books etc. on basic investment knowledge.

Use that knowledge to acquire property/equities/fixed interest securities over the next six months and to increase your income streams by adding a new income stream each year. Intend having your own business fully operational within two years and having more than six months worth of cash available to handle any possible shortfalls.

Increase your income by 20 per cent so that it doubles every 3.6 years, be strategic in your spending, manage your portfolio actively to realise a minimum yield of 15 per cent and be tax effective with all investments and personal income.

4. Use Vision and Your Creative Spirit Through Your Imagination to Create Ideas and to Design Your Life.

Most people work too hard to make a living. You need five minutes each day for quiet visualisation, to imagine and reinvent yourself so that you have an empowering life.

Ask yourself, 'What am I grateful for?', 'Who loves me?', 'Who do I love?' and 'What is my purpose?'

5. Take Massive Action about your Intention and Goals.

Make yourself take at least one small step each day towards your outcome, no matter how small the step.

At the end of the day you must ask the power questions, 'What did I achieve today?' and 'How much closer to my goal am I?'

To recap, the five magic steps are:
- Know exactly where you are right now.
- Focus upon a specific intention.
- Have a specific game plan to deliver your intentions.
- Use vision and your creative spirit through your imagination to create ideas and to design your life.
- Take massive action about your intention and goals.

There is no right or wrong, only outcomes.

Some people would rather be right than happy.

Roy McDonald

The Seven Year Plan

∽

'The man who actually knows what he wants in life has already gone a long way toward attaining it.'

Napoleon Hill

29 The Seven Year Plan

I have created a seven year plan, which has at its foundation, very deep, strong beliefs that build a very solid structure leading to the *long-term financial success* I believe you desire and deserve.

We must move towards the fundamentals of financial success, and have an understanding of what the process is all about.

If we look at financial success, it's very simple and is based, like all great things, on very simple technologies.

For instance, every great piece of music was created from just seven notes and variations between those seven notes. How they are mixed is what creates the masterpiece. All great paintings are made up of three basic colours and the tiny variations between them. Every great book written in the English language came from the 26 letters in the alphabet and a few thousand words carefully organised.

There are 30,000 diet books on the market right now, but you could boil those 30,000 books down to six basic diet plans, and then you could boil those six basic plans down to three fundamentals, which are:

- Right attitude
- Right nutrition
- Right exercise.

We can also simplify financial success. Let's focus on the 80/20 rule—the 'Pareto Principle'—discovered a few hundred years ago. It simply says that 80 per cent of what we do only produces 20 per cent of the result. Obviously, that's a very important result and it is only a very small part.

In my opinion, however, our effectiveness is really restricted to 20 per cent of what we do, which produces a total of 80 per cent of our overall results.

> 'The person who makes a success of living is the one who sees his goal steadily and aims for it unswervingly.'
> Cecil B de Mille

We must focus on doing the most effective work - identified in the 20 percent band - to produce the 80 percent result, and putting 100 percent effort into that 20 percent.

Looking after financial success is contingent upon sound time management. I believe time management can be simplified to one basic rule - you've got to procrastinate.

Now, I know that sounds outrageous yet, if you could procrastinate and stop doing 80 percent of your work to get 20 percent outcome - and, instead, spend your time focusing on the 20 percent effective work time - you would be much better off in all areas of your life.

An important strategy for success in this area is to have well - focused goals.

I have spent most of my life working on goals and believe I have a very good understanding of how to achieve them, because I get consistent results.

What I have learned, however, is that goals are only a beginning, and in fact are an outcome we wish to achieve. What is more important is to have intention, and what is more important than intention is purpose.

If you have absolute purpose in your life, intention follows very simply and goals always fill the space, to deliver the purpose.

This is the important question always to ask yourself: 'Is what I am doing now moving me towards my goals?' If the answer is 'yes' you continue, if the answer is 'no' you stop.

Most people believe the fundamental secret to financial freedom is achieving riches in your life, and to do that all you need to do is become financially free—in other words, have enough money.

Would that be right?

My belief is that's actually not true. In fact, I've observed this for many years and I've dealt with literally thousands of clients and discovered that they often increased their income and did not necessarily become any happier. In fact, they appeared to need even more money as time went on—

as their income grew they spent at the rate they were earning.

Has this been true in your life? Can you remember back to the first income you ever had? Can you remember what happened? Can you remember thinking 'if only I could get an extra $10,000 then everything would start to work?' If this is true for you, then maybe this is a secret worth knowing.

> **When the student is ready, the teacher will appear.**
>
> **When the teacher is ready, the student will appear**

My belief is that income has very little to do with wealth. It is important, as it is the river of gold as described in *The Richest Man in Babylon*, but without the aspects of care and planning it doesn't matter how much money you earn, you won't have enough.

To complete your Seven Year Plan, (see Figure 8) you need to begin with the end in mind.

Go seven years in advance and write down in the space provided, what it is that you would like as an outcome. For instance under Business/Career, you might write in, "I have created three different businesses, one in property, one in food and one dealing with a distribution system through the Internet". At this point these are generally concepts, ideas, that you are putting out as an intention to the Universe.

My Seven Year Plan

Name: _____ Date: _____

Begin with the end in mind. Go straight to the year 2014/15 and fill it in, then work backwards to this year.

	2008/09	2009/10	2010/11	2011/12	2012/13	2013/14	2014/15
5 Forms of Income							
Business/ Career							
Investment/ Property							
Equities/Shares							
Personal Development							
Relationships/ Family							
Children							
Health							
Intellectual							
Social							
Spiritual							
Other…							

Figure 8

Then work backwards to see the steps that are required in the years in between; from then till now.

You will never have any challenges with filling in what you need to do if you know where you are going.

If you would like to print the seven year plan, go to *www.onelife.com.au/freedom* or use Figure 8 in this book. If you do download the form, you can type your responses directly into the document.

What is important is that you fill this in.

When we work with clients over seven years, we have our seven year plan which is designed to take their plan even further.

By way of a guide, you may wish to note the major aspects of our seven year plan, which are as follows:

- Your dreams, your destiny—decisions and goal setting
- How to get what you really want—pain, pleasure and mental state
- The power to create and the power to destroy beliefs
- Questions are the answer—are you asking the right questions?
- Change is inevitable, growth is optional—the signs of successful conditioning
- The language of success—the power of transformational language and the use of metaphors
- How to use your action signals—emotions
- The ten day mental challenge—the mental challenge and the mastery system of evaluation
- Your personal compass—values and rules

- The key to an expanded life—your identity and references
- Putting it all together—health, wealth and happiness through optimum state, financial freedom, empowering relationships, vitality and well-being, time management, a code of conduct and connected spirit.

The ultimate gift is a contribution to others.

Four Traits of Highly Effective People.

There are four things that highly effective people do, which allow for their lives to be full and happy.

1. They love what they do and have passion. If they weren't making money, they would probably be tempted to do it for free.

2. Their daily activities are extremely important to them, so their values are the foundation of their existence and success.

3. They are talented at what they do. They have ability and their ability makes them one of the best in the area of activity in which they are involved.

4. They have a sense of destiny—that what they are doing is what they were born to do. They are making a unique contribution—it is almost a spiritual thing. They are 'on purpose' in what they are doing.

Questions to Ask Yourself.

Take some time out to consider where you currently are with your work, roles and family.

- Does what I am doing move me towards my goals?
- Do I love what I am doing?
- Am I good at what I am doing?
- Is it important to me?
- Is it what I was born to do?
- What was I passionate about between the ages of 7 and 14 years?

Your Compelling Future.

This process is not necessary for you to discover the meaning of life, but it's more of an exercise for you to uncover or discover the meaning of your life. It is a direction to look at the talent that you have, and to focus on this talent because your vocation should be your vacation. Your career or life path should be a lifestyle.

There is nothing worse than spending your life moving in the wrong direction. Climbing a mountain, only to find it is the wrong mountain. Clearing the jungle (as Stephen Covey says) only to discover you are in the wrong jungle. Or climbing the ladder which is leaning against the wall, only to discover that it is leaning against the wrong wall.

All these can be amazing discoveries to people. If you begin

Your life will only work when you take full responsibility for your choices. Your choice of vocation is at the top of the list.

with the end in mind and go for what you want in life, then life will always deliver, and you must be absolutely clear on what it is you want.

When you are 'on purpose' it is like your favourite dessert. You always make room for it. It's never hard work, it's always ease and grace. When you are 'on purpose' nothing stops you. You are never distracted, there is never a problem, there are never obstacles, disappointments or negative thoughts or feelings which divert you. You just 'go for it'.

These should be your goals, or your intention or your purpose. If you don't want to be a multi-multi-multi-millionaire, that's okay. You can have an objective just to be comfortable financially. As long as there is enough motivation with that, then that is what you will get.

The Universe has no favourites. Your success and happiness depend on natural laws and principles – and how you use them.

Being wealthy is quite simple. In fact, how to create wealth is very, very simple to understand, but is not easy to implement. It takes commitment, dedication, time and effort, and if your only reason for getting started is that you want to be rich, that may not be compelling enough.

You'll often need some extra motivation, and you may not be prepared to pay the necessary price (and it's not all to do with money—it's sometimes just to do with focus). It is vital to have a compelling reason.

For me, my compelling reason is my two beautiful children—Harrison and Jessica...What is your compelling reason?

> **A good teacher never strives to explain her vision; she simply invites you to stand before her and see for yourself**
>
> **The Rev. R. Inman**

30 Buying Real Estate

Purchasing real estate is without doubt one of the most important decisions we can make. You need an excellent plan, and I have devised an eight step program to help you. Most profit is made in real estate from the way it is purchased: through the negotiations of terms and financing and the negotiated purchase price.

Visualise your Long-Term Intention.
In other words, determine where it is you want to live. It is important to miss out as much as possible on many of the 'stepping stone' type approaches to buying real estate, particularly for your own home, as it is very expensive.

Build a Short-Term Action Plan.
This may involve boosting your income, saving as much cash as you can, investing it for the short term and using different methods for creating wealth. Remember, control is more important than ownership.

Decide on the Target Territory.
The first thing is to know your values in the area. Do your homework. Don't listen to people's opinions, have regard for them, but look for and seek the facts.

What someone's asking price is to sell a property is one thing; what they actually sell it for is another. Don't be in a hurry. Do your homework.

Activate your System for Finding Highly Motivated sellers.

These are sellers who are more flexible on price and on terms.

Look at what is motivating a seller to sell. It could be money problems, management problems, people who have been transferred with their job, people who have invested from another state, people who have just lost their jobs, family break-ups, rental properties which have become vacant, properties which have been inherited—the list goes on and on.

In a city the size of Sydney, with a population of more than four million people, more than 20,000 owners each year will default on their loan payments or be behind for one reason or another, and will be under some financial stress. About 2,500 of these properties will actually be foreclosed on, and many more will be sold at substantial discounts just before the foreclosure sale.

The Australian Bureau of Statistics advises us that in the year 2004—2005 25,695 people migrated from New South Wales to other states and 165,216 people migrated to New South Wales from overseas, so the opportunities are enormous. In New South Wales in 2004, there were 15,007 divorces, 5,971 bankruptcies, and 46,440 deaths.

In other words, there are lots of things happening and people need to find a buyer for their properties.

Let's look at the morality of this. In the case of a property being on the market due to the owners' misfortune, some people could say that you were taking advantage of their problems.

Actually, it's just the opposite. These people need their problems solved, and they need them solved quickly. The longer it takes the more it will cost them, and the more it will become a burden to them. They will often be very grateful for someone to come and take a property off their hands.

There are nine access systems which you need to activate to locate the properties:

- Newspaper classified advertisements
- Real estate agents
- Your own sphere of influence
- Looking by wandering around
- Banks and lending institutions
- Your own direct advertisements
- Direct mail
- Exchange and investment clubs
- Other professionals, e.g. accountants, finance brokers, insurance agents, etc.

There are four processes you will need to go through to acquire a property, and the steps are:

- Find the lead (Internet, RP Data, Newspaper/Real Estate Agent/Private Sale, etc)
- Complete a 'bargain finder' (I will explain later)

- 💲 Write an offer to buy
- 💲 Buy the property.

You might need to look at between 50 and 100 properties to find one property owner under these circumstances. It's like mining for gold—you need to look through a lot of dirt to find the gold. You will be paid a minimum of $100 per hour for doing this kind of work.

How did I work this out? If you can save $10,000, and spend 100 hours (two hours each week for a year) doing it, then it works out to $100 per hour. You must stay motivated and you must be ready to move.

Just to come back to the 'bargain finders' you are looking for:

1. A motivated seller
2. A good location
3. Good financing
4. Good condition
5. Good price

Analyse Each Property for Value.

You need a scoring system to appraise the five aspects of the 'bargain finder'. The scoring system would be from 1 to 10, where 1 is low and 10 is excellent. If the property scores less than 25 points, I would pass on the property.

Complete the Physical Inspection of the Property After you have Scored It.

Ask as many questions as you need to in order to make

sure you are happy with the property. Don't be worried about them trying to put you off or just wanting you to have a quick look—ask lots of questions. Don't hesitate to ask outright if the owner is flexible enough to negotiate the price or the terms.

Always remember, the first person to mention a number loses. Let them do most of the talking, you ask all the questions.

Negotiate the Deal

This is an extremely important area, and some people are not necessarily very skilled in this area. A master negotiator is always friendly, fair and flexible. Most people believe that in purchasing you have to be the opposite; however, the objective is to have a win-win situation.

It's not about being such a good person that you give money away, it's about knowing what you want, what you are prepared to pay and holding the position. It is also about being flexible regarding some of the possible solutions for the other party so that they can win as well.

The other way of doing it is through intimidation, competition and inflexibility. These usually don't work, particularly on a long-term basis.

The challenge of life is to appreciate everything and attach yourself to nothing.

A couple of tips:
- Always act like it is not important whether you buy this property or not
- Know exactly what your outcome is going to be and what you are looking for
- Make sure you gain rapport with the seller, that they understand exactly where you are coming from and what your motivation is, and that you understand what their motivation is.

How you Buy the Property can be as Important as how Much you Pay for it, if not more so.

To maximise your time use the following program:
- Never look at a property until you have scored it and it has scored in excess of 25 points
- Let your fingers do the walking
- Don't get emotionally involved with the property.

The terms can be more important than the price. Buying with no deposit or without spending money on legals can make your purchase very simple financially, and give you enormous yield and flexibility.

There are a number of techniques to do this:
- Absolutely no deposit at all, only a second mortgage
- A blanket mortgage on other property
- Lease options
- The 'A.B.C. technique'—Anything But Cash
- The 'O.P.R. technique'—Other People's Resources.

Other techniques:

💲 Negotiate with a real estate agent on their fees

💲 Negotiate the lowest interest rates you can get—1 per cent interest on a $100,000 loan is $1,000 a year. On a 20 year loan, this will amount to in excess of $35,000.

> **FOUR THINGS TO REMEMBER WHEN BUYING REAL ESTATE:**
>
> 1. Use the least amount of money possible.
>
> 2. The least amount of risk possible
>
> 3. The shortest possible time to complete the transaction
>
> 4. Make the largest amount of money possible

> Love All, Need Nothing, Serve All.
>
> Roy McDonald

The Psychology of Winning

~

Attitude
Habits
Self-Image
Desire
Change
Creativity
Confidence

Attitude

~

*'The greatest discovery of this generation
is that we can alter our lives
by altering our attitude of mind.'*

William James

31 Attitude

How does your attitude impact on the following categories:
- Health and Vitality
- Family and Friends
- Financial Matters
- Business/Career
- Intellectual Development
- Social Development
- Personal Development
- Spiritual Life
- Contribution to the Community

What is the cost/gain of staying where you are? Most of us want to change our results. In fact, that is the reason we look for answers and solutions in our life.

Our results start firstly with a decision, which is a thought. What brings about this thought is a feeling. These feelings create actions, and in turn those actions create the results.

I learnt from Anthony Robbins that the source of all emotions is a combination of three forces or patterns. These patterns or forces are physiology, language and beliefs/focus. Today, you could notice the patterns that you run in your physiology, your language and your beliefs/focus.

These, in turn, will cause emotions which are the drivers. These will create a behaviour - which is an effect - and, ultimately, the results/consequences in your life.

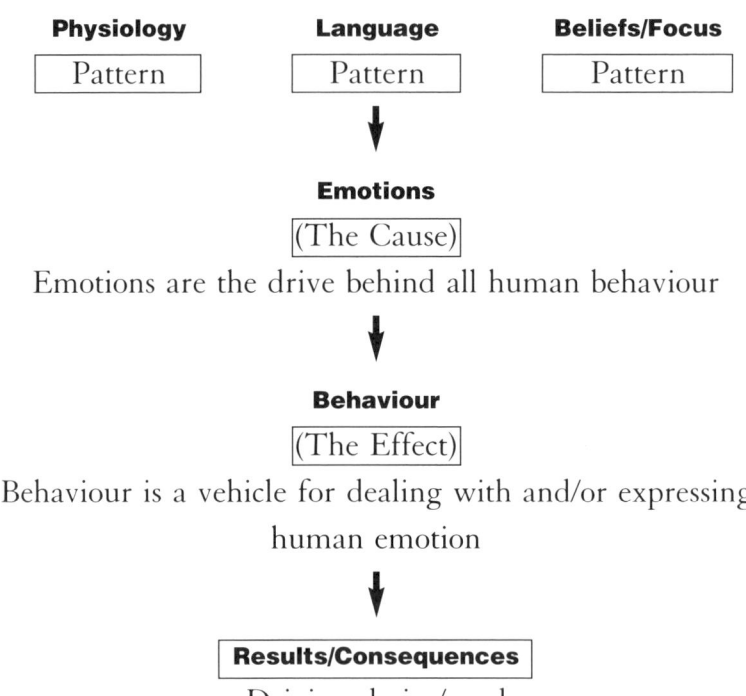

Source: Anthony Robbins

A self-confident attitude is the most important asset one can possess.

You create your environment—mental, emotional and physical—by the attitude you develop.

Attitudes are nothing more than habits of thought... and habits can be acquired.

We are either the masters or the victims of our attitudes. It's a matter of personal choice... blessing or curse.

Every change in human attitude must come through internal understanding and acceptance. Human Beings are the only known creatures who can re-shape and re-mould themselves by altering their attitudes.

The supreme test of self-motivation lies in the degree to which you develop healthy attitudes towards yourself and your circumstances.

A positive mental attitude is rooted in clear, calm and honest self-confidence.

> **Your mental attitude is something you can control outright, and you must use self discipline until you create a positive mental attitude—your mental attitude attracts to you everything that makes you what you are.**
> **Napoleon Hill**

When you truly understand yourself, your attitude will reflect that understanding.

Your attitude, not your aptitude, is the chief determinant of your success.

You are where you are and what you are because of the thoughts that dominate your mind.

32 Habits

We first form habits; then habits form us. In the individual drive towards a successful future, if we do not consciously form good habits we will unconsciously form bad ones. It is just as easy to form the habit of succeeding, as it is to succumb to the habit of failure.

The harvest we reap in our lives is measured by the attitudes and habits we cultivate.

Habits aren't instincts, they are acquired reactions. They do not just happen, they are caused. Once you determine the original cause of a habit, it is within your power either to accept or to reject it.

Using psychology, you can influence your environment and focus on thoughts. If you do so consciously and with high purpose, you can change your attitudes and, therefore, change your habits for the better.

To know the true reality of yourself, you must be aware of your conscious thoughts and also of your unconscious prejudices, biases and habits.

Every successful person has formed the habit of doing things that failures dislike doing and will not do.

Anyone can live heroically and successfully for one day. That one day then becomes the pattern for all the days of your life.

Good work habits help develop an internal toughness and a self-confident attitude that sustain you through every adversity and temporary discouragement.

> *I am your constant companion.*
> *I am your greatest helper or heaviest burden.*
> *I will push you onward or drag you down to failure.*
> *I am completely at your command.*
> *Half the things you do, you might just as well turn over to me and I will be able to do them quickly and correctly.*
> *I am easily managed - you must merely be firm with me.*
> *Show me exactly how you want something done and after a few lessons, I will do it automatically.*
> *I am the servant of all great men and women;*
> *and alas, of all failures as well.*
> *Those who are great, I have made great.*
> *Those who are failures, I have made failures.*
> *I am not a machine, though I work with all the precision of a machine plus the intelligence of a woman or a man.*
> *You may run me for profit or for ruin - it makes no difference to me.*
> *Take me, train me, be firm with me, and I will place the world at your feet.*
> *Be easy with me and I will destroy you. WHO AM I?*
>
> *I AM YOUR HABITS*
>
> **Anonymous**

33 Self-Image

> **As long as you believe something in your life is a disaster, it will unfold as a continuing disaster.**

Personality consists of numerous ideas which are more or less consistent; at the centre of all those ideas is your concept of yourself.

A wholesome self-image is vital to success. This does not mean conceit or a super-inflated ego; instead a wholesome self-respect and recognition of the human potential that exists within.

You should have respect for yourself. You need make no excuse for living or for taking up space in a world you were destined to conquer and have dominion over.

It is a psychological fact that people act like the sort of person they think they are. It's impossible for them to act otherwise for any period of time, no matter how much will power they exercise. You cannot do anything in a positive way while holding generally negative feelings about yourself. You must learn to feel that you are worthy and significant.

A low self-image forms an invisible ceiling that stops a person from attempting to rise or progress above self-imposed limitations.

34 Desire

Desire makes winners in every walk of life. The degree of success you achieve depends on the amount of sincere desire you have.

The strength of genuine desire makes you go through a challenge when other people go around it.

Desire arms you with the courage to say to yourself, 'I'm great; and I'm becoming even better!'

Less successful people say, 'I'm not as bad as a lot of other people.'

Desire develops and engenders respect for those in authority; a lack of desire breeds resentment.

Desire fosters the sense of job responsibility. Lack of desire is expressed in, 'I only work here.'

The flame of active desire carries with it the courage of your deepest convictions. You can stand up and be counted for the things that matter.

Every great religion, philosophy, invention or work of art had its creative beginning in the mind of one with desire.

> Every 'disaster' in your life is not so much a disaster, as a situation waiting for you to change your mind about it.

Desire is the perfect mental antidote for fear, despair, resentment and jealousy.

Five Natural Laws of Power

1. Power is evenly present.
2. Power cannot do for you what it can only do through you.
3. What you give away you will always get back.
4. The only limit of Power is the form through which it flows.
5. The only thing to flow into your life is that which flows out of your life.

NOTES

Change

'Actually, it matters little what the past has been, except for the lessons we have learned from it. Our prime concern should be the necessary changes we must make to create a happy and successful future.'

Paul J Meyer

35 Change

Every person can change the world by changing who they are and what they bring to the world. Everyone has been richly endowed by a generous creator that gives you the power to change yourself.

If you stubbornly resist change, you will live a single, uneventful life - no matter how serene it may be. If you welcome and accept change, you will live many lives - all equally rewarding.

> **Your mission in life is not to change the world. Your mission is to change yourself. There are no 'outside' solutions, only 'inside' solutions.**

All things change, except the fact of changing. People who don't change—who refuse to recognise change—who think so small they can't change—have provided the world with a lot of statistics and very little else.

Change is a compelling motivation to create something new, to reach for a shining star, no matter how elusive it may be. Those who seek constructive change have hungry minds. And whenever their hunger is strongest, the world improves a little.

Neither fear nor resist change . . . cultivate it. Day by day, hour by hour, concentrate on being who you want to be.

You and I, all of us, live and work in a world largely of our own making. And every aspect of our separate worlds reflect our individual fears, attitudes, thoughts and habits. The only way you can change your world is to change your mind. Grow we must—and the dynamic of human growth is change.

NOTES

36 Creativity

Here are a few characteristics of creative individuals. How many of these fit your personality?
- Optimistic about the future.
- Constructive discontent with status quo.
- Highly curious and observant.
- Open to alternatives.
- Daydreamer, projecting into the future.
- Adventurous with multiple interests.
- Ability to recognise and break bad habits.
- Independent thinker.
- Whole-brain thinker (innovative ideas into practical solutions).

Are you right or left brain dominant?

a. Is your workspace neat and orderly? Your car? Your garage?
b. Do you prefer to complete one task before starting another?
c. Do you like to talk things out at the time they occur?
d. Do you like many varieties of foods, desserts, restaurants and do you eat at a variety of times?
e. Do you usually watch TV at certain times and prefer a routine of certain programs?

f. Are your weekends full of new activities and rarely the same?
g. Do you like art, soft music and jigsaw puzzles?

If you answered yes to **a, b, c** and **e**; and no to **d, f** and **g**, you may have left-brain dominance. If you answered yes to **d, f** and **g**; and no to **a, b, c** and **e**, you may have more right brain activity.

Any conclusions? No, just more awareness!

> **The thing always happens that you believe in; and the belief in a thing makes it happen.**
> **Frank Lloyd Wright**

Don't fall in love with an invention or an idea. Ideas are expendable and there is always a new and better one.

Challenge yourself to make your ideas work and put them to practical use.

Learn a relaxation technique that works for you. Your creative imagination can be 'pre-played' and 're-played' best when you are relaxed because the left brain dominance is less intense and the right brain is receptive to your visual, and certain audio, suggestions. There are CDs that describe passive relaxation, progressive muscle relaxation, deep breathing and biofeedback techniques.

Try a few different methods until you find the one you like.

When you visualise yourself 'in the present' as if you were already accomplishing one of your goals, make certain your visual image is as you would see it out of your own eyes, not 'watching you do it' through the eyes of a spectator.

Don't scold or berate yourself with left brain criticism when you make a mistake. Develop an affirmative statement (about five words in length) describing your correct performance, in the present tense. Relax, listen to yourself state the affirmation and visualise the accompanying action and feeling.

> **When you fight life, life always wins.**

To recognise and approach problems creatively, it is best to view all problems as situations needing improvement; temporary inconveniences and opportunities to grow—to change your view or attitude toward problems. (Note: The left brain calls things problems whereas the right brain calls things challenges.)

Talking about ideas and plans needs to be balanced by trying them out. Theory and practice converge into wholeness. Field test your ideas.

When approaching any decision, consider using the technique which Benjamin Franklin said was his standard method for decision making. Put two column headings on a piece of paper, marked 'advantages' and 'disadvantages'.

In the advantages column, list all benefits and positive results you would receive if you were to go forward with your decision. List all of the disadvantages and potential consequences of your decision in the second column. Study the possible impact of the advantages and disadvantages. If the advantages outweigh the disadvantages, and if you can live with the consequences and positive benefits, then go forward with your decision.

Take time out to ride your bike, build sand castles, fly a kite, smell a rose, walk in the woods or barefoot in the sand.

We adults need to explore the wonderful, right brain world of the creative child within. (Do it this weekend!)

Questions About your Creativity:

- Do you fantasise and imagine your own success? How recently have you done this?
- Do you encourage or criticise yourself in your self-talk? Have you made up a brief statement or affirmation to use when your self-talk becomes negative?
- Do you replay or rehash past failures? Are they more vivid in your replay than your successes?
- Do you replay or reinforce past successes? Do you visualise these successes through your own eyes? Do you see yourself as a real winner in life? How can this attitude help achieve your goals?

Confidence

∼

'All of the truly successful people I've ever known had one quality or characteristic in common; a high degree of personal self-confidence—a healthy self-image.'

Paul J Meyer

37 Confidence

Unshakable confidence is the sense of certainty we all want. The only way you can consistently experience confidence, even in environments and situations you've never previously encountered, is through the power of faith.

Imagine and feel certain about the emotions you deserve to have now, rather than wait for them to spontaneously appear some day in the far distant future.

When you're confident, you're willing to experiment, to put yourself on the line.

One way to develop faith and confidence is simply to practice using them. If I were to ask whether you're confident that you can tie your own shoes, I'm sure you could tell me with perfect confidence that you can. Why? Only because you've done it thousands of times! So, practice confidence by using it consistently, and you'll be amazed at the dividends it reaps in every area of your life.

> 'I suggest that if you firmly imprint your expectations onto the Universe your yellow brick road will appear in front of you, as if by magic.'
> **Simon Hall**

In order to get yourself to do anything, it's imperative to exercise confidence rather than fear. The tragedy of many people's lives is that they avoid doing things because they're afraid; they even feel bad about things in advance. Remember: the source of success for outstanding achievers often finds its origins in a set of nurtured beliefs for which that individual had no references!

The ability to act on faith is what moves the human race forward.

Confidence is a feeling, which is created when the soul and the spirit connect.

When you feel confident, you are in harmony with the Universe. Confidence gives you strength, with style.

When you are confident you know - and you know that you know; you know why you know.

Confidence generates a non-physical aura which captures the conscious attention of everyone in your presence, and for that they will admire you.

Confidence sets off a vibration which causes others to trust your ability. It instills in them a feeling of safety when following your lead.

Everyone has confidence. You may not have it where you want it or when you want, but you've got it!

Confidence is the feeling which comes when you know you can.

You are not born with confidence; however, anyone can develop confidence if they are willing to pay the price.

Confidence is absolutely essential if you are going to lead a totally free life. Confidence will permit you to live your heart's desire.

Understanding your relationship with the ever present, all knowing, all powerful Spirit will give you the confidence that you can be, do or have whatever you dream, even though you don't know how it will materialise—that confidence comes from the faith in the lawful working of Spirit.

Confidence is your passport to a fun-filled, exciting new life. Lack of or no self-confidence causes a person's life to be filled with doubt and fear.

Frustration is caused by people denying their heart's desire. Your heart's desire is for greater good in your life.

There is only one Universal Mind. All people are an expression of one infinite power. Your mind and Albert Einstein's are the one Mind.

The only differences between people are appearance and results. We all have the same potential. You will never seriously want to be, do, or have anything beyond your capabilities.

Churchill's demonstration of confidence in his famous speech provides a great model to emulate—'Never, never, never, never, never give up'.

Confident people never permit failures to reverse their growth pattern, nor do they permit other people's criticism to deflect them.

Confidence is feeling at home with yourself. You've got to be your own best friend. Know that you are good enough—that you are better than good enough!

Every morning before you rise, go to that place known to only a few—the strong, the tough, the best—connect and prepare for the day:

- Check your self-image—see yourself as a star
- Develop your strength and manage your weakness
- Look for the good in everyone.

Self-Confidence

Self-confidence can be gained only through practical know-how; know-how comes from knowledge and experience; and experience can be gleaned only through a willingness to confront obstacles and situations that others ordinarily fear.

The real secret of successful people is the absolute confidence that they have in themselves and their abilities.

Confidence in yourself gives you a clear vision of your goal and creates desire that is strong enough to sweep away all obstacles.

Real confidence in yourself is always demonstrated by action. When you possess self-confidence, you are master of others because you are master of yourself.

Confidence in yourself is the key to all achievement. It reinforces ability, doubles energy, expands mental facilities, and increases your personal power.

To think confidently—act confidently. Act the way you want to feel.

Five Self-Confidence Building Exercises:

- Be a front seater—sitting up the front builds confidence
- Practice making eye contact—how a person uses their eyes says a lot about their confidence
- Walk 25 per cent faster—people who demonstrate super confidence walk faster than the average person
- Practice speaking up—the more you speak up, the more you add to your self-confidence
- Smile big—a smile is excellent medicine for confidence deficiency. It melts away opposition, instantly.

To become confident, think, act and be confident. You should also say to yourself: 'I am confident, I am a really confident person.'

Seventeen Success Principles

~

*'The harvest we reap in our lives is measured
by the attitudes and habits we cultivate.'*

Napoleon Hill

38 Seventeen Success Principles

1. A Positive Mental Attitude.
2. Definiteness of Purpose.
3. Going the Extra Mile.
4. Accurate Thinking.
5. Self-Discipline.
6. The Master Mind.
7. Applied Faith.
8. A Pleasing Personality.
9. Personal Initiative.
10. Enthusiasm.
11. Controlled Attention.
12. Teamwork.
13. Learning from Defeat.
14. Creative Vision.
15. Budgeting Time and Money.
16. Maintaining Your Health.
17. Using Cosmic Habit Force.

39 The Step-by-Step Approach to Turning $1 into $1 Million in Seven Years or Less, $1 at a Time

The most important thing in this process is your ability to create wealth; and, first you need to create a reason. This could be your children, or any other reason you feel passionate about.

To create $1M you need five forms of income. These are:

- Job—you need a job; if you don't have one, get one.
- Trading—there are two parts to this; trading property and trading cfds, options and futures (*Momentum Trading for Success*). There are great possibilities to build up cash quickly in these areas.

- Business building.
- 'Buy and hold' income/growth investments.
- Create a business you don't work in.

You get paid for the value that you add.
- See what others are doing and model them.
- Use all natural laws.
- Use a money partner, someone you can enroll into the transactions you are doing.
- Use lenders.
- Sell things, e.g. Have a garage sale.
- Sell ideas.

You must spend less than you earn.
- Develop a Strategic Spending Plan. You can't move to second base if you haven't got to first. All first bases must be completed.
- Save 10 per cent (minimum) into a wealth account.

You must increase your wealth.
- Minimise your tax.
- Invest with diversity; spread your risk.
- Asset allocation.
- Gearing and Leverage.
- Compound rates of return (eg a smoker who gives up for 40 years, 1 pack a day at 10 per cent yield will save $2m).

You must protect your wealth.
- Corporate Trustees.

💲 Insurance—life/income/property/superannuation. If you are a single person with no dependents you may not need life insurance. If you have dependents you need term life insurance (preferably through a superannuation fund, which is tax deductible) and you need income protection.

💲 Use options. Control is more important than ownership.

Enjoy your wealth—what's the point of having it if you don't enjoy it?

💲 Lifestyle is everything.

💲 Share your wealth.

You must have a seven year plan.

💲 Written goals—short–medium–long term.

💲 Abundance vs scarcity.

Remember: *You* are your greatest asset. So you must invest in yourself. *If you don't, nobody else will!*

If these basic strategies are in place you will surely succeed:

💲 Create a reason.

💲 Five forms of income—a new form each year.

💲 Strategic spending plan.

💲 Save at least 10 per cent into a wealth account.

💲 Minimise your tax.

💲 Written goals—short–medium–long term.

YOU are your greatest asset!

Turn $1 into $1 million

Use gap technology in your seven year plan: know where you are now, know where you want to go, and fortify the gap between where you are and where you want to go.

Year 1	$1 - $20,000
Year 2	- $40,000
Year 3	- $80,000
Year 4	- $160,000
Year 5	- $320,000
Year 6	- $640,000
Year 7	- $1,280,000

Do you know where to start?

Whatever your present position, no matter how good or how bad, that is where you should start.

To get the first $20,000 you need to:

- Save it.
- Borrow it.
- Increase your income (e.g. in your job).
- Create other income.

Remember, the first $20,000 will be the hardest to get, as you must learn many skills to get to first base.

Some Strategies Worth Considering:

1. The better the idea, the better the money you make.
2. Start where you are: fix up your debt—you may need to consolidate all your debts into one affordable repayment.

See if the debt can legally be converted into a tax deduction.

3. For all the things you want, create a business for them. For example, if you want to travel, create an importing business. When you travel your trips can become a tax deduction.

If you want a boat, start a business renting out boats. Arrange leasing finance to purchase the boats so there is no capital cost to you. Renting out your boats will give you income and a tax deduction for the lease payments.

4. Sell anything that won't grow in value or will take a long time to return a profit, especially if you are emotionally attached to it.

5. Follow your heart and your passion. Create a lifestyle, a profit and a tax deduction—in that order.

6. The purpose to being abundantly successful is to give you more life. The purpose of having a business is to get more life; not to give your life to the business. The purpose of having a business is to buy you the real estate that you want to operate from. The mortgage interest payment should be tax deductible, as should be the rent, so why not own as opposed to renting it.

7. Create a home office, so you can get really organised and create a possible tax deduction at the same time. This tax deduction should include your home computer, phone, internet connection etc.

8. Rent a house that has development possibilities, with an option to buy in 12 months at an agreed price, with permission to sub-let and vendor's approval to lodge a development application to the council.

9. There are many more strategies I am sure you can think of. These are just a few to start with. NB: You must run a business that is legitimate—it must create assessable income and deductible expenses that are correctly and precisely accounted for.

Your job is to move from wherever you are at this moment, e.g. $1 to $20,000, $20,000 to $40,000, $40,000 to $80,000, etc.

- Within 3 years, sixty per cent of your income is to come from businesses (people working for you) and investments (money working for you).
- By Year 2 start taking one day off work (job).
- By Year 3 take two days off work and replace the time doing something you love to do—follow your passion.
- Within 5 years 100 per cent of your income is to come from businesses and investments.

Bottom Line

If you don't commit to doing the basics such as reading your goals each day, creating your wealth account, saving a minimum of ten per cent from all incomes, completing your strategic plan and reviewing your seven year plan in the next six months (focusing on your outcome), all the other strategies, tools and techniques won't matter.

Remember: If you want to get to home base you must go to 1st, 2nd and 3rd first. If you shortcut you won't win.

THE STRATEGIES OF THE WEALTHY:

Wealthy people are not wealthy just because they invest their money wisely, they are wealthy because of how they invest their time.

1. Wealthy people invest their time in learning about financial intelligence—knowing how to play the game.

2. Wealthy People Invest Their TIME in EMOTIONAL FITNESS—Conditioning themselves to wealth, able to take a loss and recover, deal with their fears, and anger and unworthiness.

3. Wealthy people invest their time in wealth networks—Building a better garden, attracting more butterflies.

4. Wealthy people invest their time in discovering their pathway of least resistance—Focusing on where they are, being effective, adding value & leveraging themselves.

40 Summary

We have covered a variety of financial tools and techniques, including:
- The Six Masteries [Ch 12]
- Twelve Wealth Strategies [Chs 16, 18, 19]
- Twelve False Wealth Assumptions [Ch 20]
- Twelve Secrets of Wealth [Ch 14]
- How to be Debt Free in Five Years [Ch 22]
- How to be Financially Independent in Seven Years [Ch 22]
- Ten Commandments for Creating a Financial Fortress [Ch 23]
- How to Create a Cash Flow with Five Forms of Income [Ch 5]
- Your own Wealth Creation System [Chs 4, 29, 39]
- Eight Principals of Wealth [Ch 25]
- A Powerful Strategic Spending Plan [Ch 18]
- Five Secrets of Running Your own Business [Ch 26]
- Twelve Rules for Starting Your Own Business [Ch 27]
- The Five Core Elements of Your Own Business [Ch 26]
- Five Magic Steps for Achieving Your Goals [Ch 28]
- Eight Steps to Making Successful Real Estate Purchases [Ch 30]
- Nine Access Systems for Locating Profitable Real Estate [Ch 30]
- Your Seven Year Plan [Ch 29]
- Four Traits of Highly Effective People [Ch 29]
- The PIE Chart Investment Approach [Ch 9]

- How to get a minimum 30 per cent return from the government [Ch 5]
- How to be a multi-millionaire as a lifestyle [Chs 20, 28, 38]
- How to use the system to create a million dollars from one dollar a day [Ch 39]
- The psychology of winning. [Ch 31-38]

A Final Secret to Wealth:

There really are No Secrets—it's just Common Sense.

Common Sense + Action = Powerful Results

The interesting thing, however, is that sense doesn't seem to be common, particularly when it comes to consistency, focus and bringing wealth to consciousness. For the percentages to be so badly stacked against success, that is with the ninety five per cent failure rate, one can only conclude that the majority of the population is incapable of being consistent.

If you take these ideas, use the secrets of wealth and put them in action, there is nothing you can't accomplish, and that still appears to be a secret to most people.

You can succeed at anything when you focus your attention on, and are determined to work through, the layers of fears. I encourage you to move forward, consistently, towards your dreams in life.

Join the five per cent of successful people.

Life's Purpose

I know that my life purpose is greater than I can imagine,

and I know that is true for everyone.

I know there is a force in the Universe greater than I am and greater than everyone else.

If we are willing to surrender ourselves and align with this force, then we can achieve all that we can dream; we can make a difference on this planet by being a great example, being the best we can be.

I hope you access your life's purpose and achieve all your dreams for yourself and your family.

Roy McDonald

Live your life in harmony, balance and abundance, as it is your birthright!

41 Recommended Reading

Awaken the Giant Within—Anthony Robbins
Conversations With God, Book 1—Neale Donald Walsch
Everyday Enlightenment—Dan Millman
Goals—Brian Tracy
Laws of Spirit—Dan Millman
Manifest Your Destiny—Dr Wayne W. Dyer
Rich Dad's Guide to Investing—Robert T. Kiyosaki
Seeds of Greatness—Denis Waitley
The 22 Immutable Laws of Marketing—Al Ries and Jack Trout
The Journey—Brandon Bays
The Magic of Believing—Claude M. Bristol
The Magic of Thinking Big—David J. Schwartz
The New Market Wizards—Jack D. Schwager
The One Minute Manager Meets the Monkey—William Oncken Jr & Hall Burrows
The One Minute Millionaire—Mark Victor Hansen & Robert G Allen
The Power of Now—Eckhart Tolle
The Richest Man in Babylon—George S Clason
The Road Less Travelled—M. Scott Peck
The Warren Buffett Way—Robert G Hagstrom
There's a Spiritual Solution to Every Problem—Dr Wayne W Dyer
Think and Grow Rich—Napoleon Hill
You Were Born Rich—Bob Proctor
The E Myth Revisited—Michael E. Gerber

42 Programs Available

OneLife offers a variety of programs:
- ☐ **OneLife Abundance**
- ☐ **Momentum Trading for Success**
- ☐ **Trading for Profits**
- ☐ **Business Mastery**
- ☐ **Instant Property Wealth**
- ☐ **Roy's Mentoring Program**

If you would like information on any of these programs, please email **info@onelife.com.au** or phone: **1300 365 590** and one of our team will contact you.

Name: _____

Address: _____

_____ Postcode: _____

Contact Tel: _____ Best Time: _____

Email address: _____

43 Glossary

All Ordinaries Index Comprises shares of around 310 of Australia's largest listed companies.

Asset Allocation Also known as portfolio balance, it is the spreading of risk by investing in different areas.

Asset Trust A trust in which assets are held for the protection of the investor and allowing discretion for distribution.

Australian Bureau of Statistics Compiles and publishes data on subjects ranging from Australian agriculture to the financial markets.

Bank Bills A form of short term finance provided and guaranteed by a bank.

Blue Chip Shares Shares from the biggest and, generally considered, safest companies such as BHP and CSR.

Bonds A fixed interest security issued by the national or state government.

Business Risk The chance that an individual firm may fail due to bad management or outside influences.

Capital Gains Tax The tax applicable to the growth component of an investment.

Commodities A term used in the stock market to describe tradeable items such as gold or beef.

Debt Free Having absolutely NO DEBT.

Derivatives This term means that one financial product has been derived from another financial product, e.g. a 'share option'.

Direct Investment You are the sole owner of an investment property.

Discretionary Trust a trust where the trustee has discretion as to who the beneficiaries are in terms of distribution.

Dividend Yield The dividend per share (DPS) divided by the company's current share price.

Financially Independent Being able to do the things you enjoy doing irrespective of financial reward.

Inflation Indexed Bonds Either the capital value is indexed to inflation, or the interest payments are indexed to inflation.

Negative Gearing Borrowing against property or equities and the income (rent or dividends) is less than the cost of the borrowing/mortgage.

Neutral Gearing Similar to negative gearing; however, the rent or dividend is equal to the interest payment on the borrowing/mortgage.

Positive Gearing Where the rent or dividend is greater than the borrowing/ mortgage payment.

Trading Trust A trust that is formed specifically for a business venture, for the purposes of protection and flexibility

Volatility As a general rule, the longer time a bond has to run, the more volatile it is, as it is more subject to varying interest rates and bond prices.

Wealth A substantial sum of money; however, in this program wealth includes all aspects of one's life.

44 Testimonials

§ After completing the OneLife program, we were able to regain balance. The twelve months support has been fantastic. The constant reminder of the steps needed and the association with successful people has helped keep us on track. Life is great. To be able to say "YES" to our dreams, and particularly our children's dreams, is fantastic!
Christine and Ken Hawkins

§ Oh, what an awesome journey! Recently I heard 'to become passionate about your work is the last day you will ever work.' This is so right for me; my days are now spent doing what I really enjoy. These days I can't get the smile off my face; I am soaring like an eagle. Thank you to Roy and to his Team.
Jill McIntyre

§ OneLife has had a big impact on our lives. It lets us recognise when an opportunity turns up. It makes us, ultimately, better people. We love the challenge that life has to offer.
Robin Wiessel

§ The past 9 months have been an amazing personal journey. I am so grateful the Universe showed up for me as it has been my privilege and pleasure to have the powerful OneLife program in my life."
Patricia Durbin

§ I have just launched Australia's first drink bottle for dogs. The huge success of this product has captured the imagination of entrepreneurs internationally! Prior to attending the OneLife program in January 2003, I wouldn't have had the faith in myself to follow through with this idea. I'm so happy that I kept going! It has been an honour to share this part of my journey with you.
Andrew Larkey

§ I just wanted to take some time out to truly thank Roy for what I believe is his sincere desire to give and share his knowledge and beliefs and to inspire people to really live life. His brand of personal development is unique in Australia and has potential to touch and change many more lives. Thank you Roy for the contribution you have made to mine.

Suzee Brain

I am writing this with much joy and gratitude in my heart and at this point in my life I am the happiest I have ever been. One man had a dream, which has brought so much awakening, light and joy to so many lives. Thank you Roy from the bottom of my heart for following your dream and helping me realise mine.

Nicole Marie Sabadina

Roy,

After the program we set some goals together: To live and enjoy life together as a couple full-time, as I used to work 3 weeks a month away from my wife.

My goal was to begin trading in property and shares to double our monthly income (eg: June's income was $20,000).

We commenced property trading after attending the Instant Property Wealth Program and our first transaction yield was in excess of $45,000 from a property purchase of $125,000 in less than 3 months. Our second transaction is already underway.

Our income in December was $44,000 (after tax), not including any property deals.

We are now truly grateful for each other and for the knowledge we have learnt and applied from the programs we attended.

Paul and Debbie Hensley

(Property Investor & Trader)

Thanks Roy and the Team for helping me move forward in my life. Both Helen and I have grown enormously since the program.

When I first did the program in March 2001, I was an electrician working 70 hours per week, earning about $300K gross, of which I netted some $80K after all expenses, and I thought I was doing well. Within 18 months I achieved just under $1M in my business activity and halved the time that I worked to 35 hours.

In that same time, using the skills that I have learned in IPW (the real estate program), I have put together transactions in excess of $3.5M of which I could liquidate over $1M immediately.

Once again, thank you for your support and helping me to being well under way toward reaching my ultimate goal of $5M in five years.

Harry Charalambous

§ Just Do It!

I attended Roy's program over two years ago.

Two years later I am writing this letter to give my testimony as I want to help people in making the decision to do the program.

I assure you that this program works. In brief a few results I have achieved:

· In the first year, my taxation bill was reduced by over $20,000.

· In the second year my taxation bill was reduced by a further $10,000.

I have started to trade in futures. In three months I have made 40% profit.

This year I have invested in property and have made a capital gain of $70,000.

Two years later I strongly believe that doing the program was the right choice. I have had excellent financial results. I have also benefited much more in other aspects of my life as I am now happy and focused and look with optimism and certainty into the future.

I wish every one of you success and I am absolutely sure that you can achieve your dreams.

I have to honestly repeat:
"Just Do It!"
Good Luck!

Adam
(IT Manager)

§ I was earning $65,000 when I did the program. Now I am a millionaire with several forms of income & enjoy the rewards of controlling my own investments. I am very grateful for the opportunities that the program has opened up for me & which turned my life around.

Geoff Bednal

§ Since doing the program my confidence has grown tenfold & so has my income! Within 2 months my income went from $100K to $150K a 50% increase & is still climbing.

Danielle Upham

§ Roy,

I would like to thank you for what my experience was at the program. My learning at the Hunter Valley Retreat has touched so many people and has had far reaching effects for my family and friends. I have recently discovered the fact that your company planted a seed of passion for growth in me and that, through daily reflection and study, I am unlocking door after door in mind and spirit (even after a year and a half) - it's a fascinating experience and I'm lucky to have people around me I can discuss it with.

Thanks again Roy and the team!

Benjamin Reid
(Computer Analyst)

§ Dear Roy and the Team,
Thank you for an amazing weekend, I learnt so much about myself.
I learnt that I need to LEAD, DELEGATE and MAKE DECISIONS in a HEART BEAT. This has given me so much insight into how I lead my company.
You have built an amazing place and an amazing team Roy. Congratulations and thank you.
Love

Debbie Hansen

§ Hello Roy and all of your wonderful staff.
What a fantastic five days this has been for me. I came into the program knowing I needed changes in my personal life and general business. I had an idea of what had to be done but not the tools to do it.
I have been searching for a while for the right group of people to reconfirm in my heart that anything is possible to achieve. I feel like a new person with unlimited potential and know that the goals I have set will not only be achieved but I will exceed them as well.
Cheers,

Tony

§ Dear Roy
I would just like to write a short letter to you, thanking both yourself and your staff for a truly life changing experience.

The program provided many thought inducing strategies which I am eager to follow through.
Regarding the MTFS program provided, Dr Claus is truly a genius and I am looking forward to this aspect of my business as it is such a portable job. (Fancy being anywhere on the planet and making money!)
I am keen to get my finances in order.
Sending you the warmest wishes.

Phill Bone
(Electrician)

Hi Roy
§ I just wanted to write this email to say thank you for an amazing program - it was totally life changing. I will never be the same again. I have already started on a new journey and am enjoying every moment.
Thanks Roy for your passion.

Kristine Haasnoot
(Trainer/ Teacher)

§ I first heard about your company at the Money Show last year & later attended an introduction night in the city. I decided to take the offer up as there was a whole program covering a wide range of financial opportunities from Real Estate to Shares and Business. All of which I had a financial interest in.

Since joining the program, I have refinanced my home and I am buying an investment unit, as well as another off the plan with a "put call option". That means in a year or so I will be selling a property and possibly moving house. There is still a lot of work and things to do and learn, however the future looks great.

Keith Nalty
(Roads & Traffic Authority)

℘ Dear Roy

I would firstly like to express my deep felt gratitude to you for providing such an inspiring and enlightening program. It was one of the greatest experiences of my life. It has exposed the self imposing limitations that have been constraining my growth.

For the first time, I am not preoccupied with worrying about money. Instead I am now confident regarding my financial future. Thank you Roy for showing me the direction to start this journey. With deep felt thanks and happiness

Frank Hasiuk.
(IT Team Leader)

℘ Dear Roy

What an amazing experience. I have searched all my life for the answer to what happens, why, how and there it was. Over the most enlightening five days of our lives. We have made numerous discoveries. We now look forward to some enormous changes, in lifestyle and attitude and for this we will remain ever grateful.
Sincerely

Eddie & Heather Cartledge
(Motel Owners)

℘ Roy

I would like to congratulate you and your team on an excellent five day program. As I have mentioned to you, I have done an Anthony Robbins program, similar in nature but I was not able to engage in that program the way that I have here.

The caring atmosphere that was promoted throughout the whole program was overwhelming. The individuals on the teams were a credit to your organization.

Mick Huggett
(Consultant)

℘ Roy,

It has been just over 12 months since completing the program.

In a short time my sales increased, my enthusiasm grew and my way of thinking on life has never been better. I wanted to drop you this brief line to thank you for such an opportunity and in my current role, have been happy to refer the Program to those needing a lift

and a pick me up for life.
All the best for your future business.
Kind Regards,
Colin Hawkins
(Real Estate Agent)

§ Roy,

Prior to completing the program we were living in Peakhurst, next door to our business, on an industrial site.

I cannot even start to explain how much of an impact the program has had on our lives.

We moved into our dream home in one month and Geoff has seen a big improvement in our business with us now saving 10% each fortnight.

Its all about being organised, totally focused on your goals, having a plan and sticking to it.

Geoff and Lisa Cummins
§ (Business Owners)

Roy,

Eighteen months ago I borrowed money from my parents to do your program.

After the program we started our wealth account straight away and it has grown from 0% (due to no income) up to 18% last month and is still growing.

We bought a furniture retail business for almost zero money down and we turned the store around and are on target to hit a sales increase of 89% on last year. In our first year we increased our net worth from zero to almost $200,000.

We have also obtained two development sites, each looking to return more than 64% after tax profit early § next year.

Darin and Amanda Currall
(Business Owners)

Roy,

I am doing Live Trading and have $1,200 profit in the Bank and another $9,000 open profit that I § could realise.

Helen Bow
(Wellbeing Mentor)

Roy,

Six months after doing the program, my income has increased by approx. 25%. One month after the program I won the Master Builders Award for Excellence in Construction, the highest award in the industry for the renovation category. As a bonus I have also lost 14 cm from my waistline and feel much fitter.

Mal Green
(Builder)

Roy,

I was earning $350,000+ from my own sales office before going to the program, however, I was not growing my business where I could earn residual income.

Following the program, I systemised my recruiting of sales people, the training programme, administrative operations, product strategy and inventory control and now have 5 offices outside my own that will earn me over $150,000 annually, even though I am not in the actual businesses myself.

I was given the opportunity to earn 50% of the profit from the businesses in Australia and New Zealand because the owner didn't have the time to manage them. Nine months later we now have 21 locations (5 in New Zealand and 16 in Australia), a 300% increase in sales volume and over 330 people in our sales force.

I will earn over $500,000 from Australia and $100,000 from New Zealand as well as continuing to earn the income from my sales office and the residual income from my outside deals. This is still growing and I have been given the opportunity to open in Singapore and the Phillipines with the same 50% profit share deal.

Ty Pedersen
(Business Owner)

Roy,

Completing the program gave me the courage to start my own carpet cleaning business, Sensational Cleaning.

Initially I outlayed $15,000 to work as a contractor for another carpet cleaning business and my income jumped from $20,000 to roughly $45,000 in nine months.

I then ventured out on my own, beginning with a casual job that provided an income of $8,000 in two months. This assisted me in getting my own business up and running and I am now making $23,000 every three months from both the casual job and my own business.

Antony Fletcher
(Business Owner)

FREE... Financial Education Workshop

"How to turn $1 into $1,000,000 in 7 Years or less"

As a special reward for reading this book Roy McDonald is giving you the unique opportunity to attend one of his Creating Financial Success Seminars free of charge.

Here you will discover a collection of his most powerful **Share & Property Trading, Tax and Business Building Strategies.**

Strategies that enabled Roy to create more than *20 companies that turn over in excess of $30 Million a year &* become a millionaire by age 28.

If you've been looking for some straight talk on how to increase income and build wealth then this could be exactly what you're looking for. *Just have a look at what you'll learn:*

Let Roy Show You How to Turn $1 into $1 Million in 7 Years...

Discover & be introduced to the step by step recipe to turn $1 into $1 Million in 7 years... *or less.*

How to Increase Your Level of Income

Do You Aspire to be Debt Free from Major Debts in 5 Years or Less?

How to increase the Yields of Investments

Learn from Roy's *40 years experience as an Investor*. Discover the many techniques he uses to increase returns.

How to be Tax Effective? (Whether you're Self Employed or PAYG).

Learn some of the strategies used by financial geniuses to legally & ethically reduce tax. *Plus:*

- *A trading method that can generate returns of 10% and more a month*

- **Why it's easier to borrow $20 million than it is to get a 20k personal loan?**

- *How some Investors make money whether the Sharemarket is going up or down?*

- **The Massive Leverage Potential of Options**

- *How to Create Complete and Absolute Financial Abundance in Your Life*

Email: info@onelife.com.au
OR simply call 1300 36 55 90 for details
(or see the following page)

A FREE WORKSHOP ON... MONEY, SUCCESS & YOU

Yes YOU! the person working 10 hours a day, 6 days a week, feeling stressed, exhausted and without energy or enthusiasm for your family and friends. Take a stand and treat yourself to this FREE workshop. One Life International will host and present Australian Author, Educator and Self-Made Millionaire, Roy McDonald introducing one of the most profound books ever written on financial freedom, showing YOU how to achieve this with balance and harmony.

On the night, Roy will discuss key aspects, including how to:

- Earn 20% more and work 20% less within 90 days
- Minimise your tax legally
- Access $150,000 with only $2,000
- Increase your wealth through Real Estate, Share Trading and Business
- Become debt free in 5 years or less
- Create a legacy for your family

Call now to book yourself into this Free workshop. Come prepared to have your ideas challenged and then to put a plan of action into place. This is your life - treat it with the respect it deserves.

CALL NOW - PLEASE PHONE 1300 365 590
FOR THE NEXT AVAILABLE EVENT

Bring this book and have it personally autographed by Roy McDonald himself

FREE

BOOK NOW! 1300 365 590
Email: info@onelife.com.au
Website: www.onelife.com.au

Fin Accounts
NOTES

Savings Accts

① Wealth Account — Should be a Cash Management Trust or similar
£30 per week

② Cash - Account — Bank A/c, daily living expns

③ O'seas A/c — Bills, Holidays, House A/c, Mavis A/c

£20 per week